NEW POWER TO LOVE

CONCENTRATED VIRILITY FOODS

WILLIAM H. LEE, R.Ph., Ph.D.

Instant Improvement, Inc.

Instant Improvement, Inc,
1160 Park Avenue
New York, New York 10128

Manufactured in the United States of America

Library of Congress Cataloging-in-Publication Data

Lee, William H.
   New power to love: concentrated virility foods.

   Bibliography: p.
   Includes index.
   1. Impotence—Nutritional aspects. 2. Impotence—
Diet therapy—Recipes. 3. Aphrodisiacs. I. Title.
RC889.L44 1987 613.9'6 87-4041
ISBN 0-941683-00-1

IMPORTANT NOTICE

This book contains material for informational and educational purposes only. It seeks to make people aware of their health needs.

If any person makes a decision to use any data found in this book, the decision rests completely with that person and his or her own doctor.

This book is not a substitute for personal medical supervision by a qualified health professional. People with health problems should consult with their physician.

Any action taken by any reader concerning therapies or individual substances rests solely with the reader and his or her doctor.

TABLE OF CONTENTS

Foreplay

"Not tonight; I have a headache."

Sound familiar?

But here's a twist you haven't heard about.

A husband, over fifty-five, was taking nitroglycerin as an aid for angina. He wasn't using tablets, because his doctor had advised him to use a patch that sticks to the skin and releases the medication in tiny amounts on a continuous basis.

One night, on a whim, the husband removed the patch and rubbed it on his penis. Nitroglycerin is a vasodilator and the result was an erection that induced visions of his youth. He called for his wife and they tussled in bed like they did in years gone by. But, when it was over, his wife developed the worst headache in the world. Nitroglycerin!

After he confessed what he had done, he had to promise never to do it again!

The prescription drug papavarine acts on muscular flaps and valves. Doctors use it before surgery to determine if the penis can function. An erection is the result of blood flowing through the arterioles into the penis. The spongy tissue, when engorged, holds the penis erect. Interesting, but erratic, since some erections do not deflate for up to twelve hours. That can be very painful.

The search for a substance that can stimulate sexual desire and sexual performance did not begin in this century. In fact, the start of that search is lost in the farthest reaches of time. The answers may be different or they may be the same; the questions, however, never vary:

- My sexual urge is lost but not forgotten. What can I take to get it back?

• Sex is not as exciting, as interesting, or as frequent as it was when I was younger. What can I take to get it back?

• I don't have the usual male-female relationship any more. What can I do to get it back?

If this is you, you are not alone. According to the *New England Journal of Medicine*, a study involving "happily married" couples revealed that seventy percent of the men responding said they had difficulty achieving erection and ejaculation! Fully half of the respondents admitted that the sex act was less enjoyable than formerly, and they were unable to relax because of fear of performing.

And this was a survey of "happily marrieds!" What kind of report would have resulted if the respondents were single men and women?

America is not alone. Sex counselors from all over the globe, reporting in other medical journals, talk about inhibitions, incapacity, lack of sex drive, and other sexual hangups. All of this in the middle of the sexual-liberation explosion! Today we no longer have to supress our natural sexual inclinations as we did at the beginning of the twentieth century; but virtually every man will, at some time, experience an episode of impotence.

Among older people, coital incidence has declined to once a week, once a month, or not at all. But this does not have to be so.

When the body is well nurished, all body systems will work at optimum performance. There are sexual foods, herbs, essential amino acids (parts of foods), and even sexual drugs to help restore the hidden virility you thought was lost but which was really only hiding.

But many doctors are not well versed in the treatment of sexual dysfunction with natural methods. Most medical doctors have not studied nutritional means of combating ills, nor have they investigated herbs and other folklore.

Balancing good nutrition with herbal application will help to increase the flow of much-needed chemicals for sexual desire, and will help the body restore itself to normality.

There is no good reason why people should not live at **peak sexual power** from puberty till the day they pass from this realm into another.

The pleasure-making pathways are intact. It's up to you to travel them again.

One Sad Note

There are men—men desperately in need of the information contained in this volume—who will actually continue to cripple themselves by thinking that it is too expensive.

I pity them, because this is what misguided men like these will do tomorrow:

- Pay up to $75.00 a shot for some "potency medicine" that will do nothing but give them a sore rear end.

- Spend hundreds of dollars in a "sex clinic," trying to learn "potency techniques"...when their sex glands may simply be starved for the proper nutrients.

- Shell out up to $2,500.00 for a "penile implant," when better results may cost pennies at their neighborhood food store.

- Give up hope completely, and bleed their bank accounts dry, because of the alcohol and drugs they need to fight their depression.

Say what you will, a man defines himself as a man because of his sexual performance. And here, in this encyclopedia, are the sexual foods, herbs, amino acids, concentrated virility foods, and even non-prescription sexual drugs to help restore the hidden virility you may have thought was lost...but which was actually only in hiding.

The pleasure-making pathways are intact. It's up to you to travel them again.

Food and Sex

Five hundred years before the birth of Christ, Hippocrates, a great physician and teacher, taught his pupils the first secret of continued good health.

"Your food shall be your medicine—and your medicine shall be your food."

It has been twenty-five hundred years since that truth was told, but even the great teacher would have been surprised at the strides that have been made in the use of food for healing.

By using food and supplements in the correct proportion, it is possible to improve your sex life!

There is an obvious connection between the mouth, food, and sex. The mouth is the first body part to experience the taste of another person. What's a kiss but a sample taste of somebody else's body?

Staff of the *British Journal of Dermatology*, November, 1984, decided to investigate the "kiss." When they had thoroughly explored this delightful human behavior, with typical British dispassionate humor they reduced the kiss to a biochemical reaction.

It appears that kissing is a tasting behavior where each partner samples the other's semio-chemicals (special elements deposited on the skin by glands in the area). If, during the kissing-tasting ritual, we like the other's biological agents, which travel through the blood stream from the mouth to the brain and settle in the erection center, then we hunger for the rest of the meal, that is, a sexual relationship.

How many times have you said to your partner, "I love you so much I could eat you up!"?

Love, sex, and food are mingled from the start. Even on a physiological basis, there is a sharing of characteristics. The moist, delicate mouth with its soft lips has much in common with its lower partner. Even to nerve endings! Nature has planted the same sensitive nerves, called Krause's end bulbs, in the penis, in the clitoris, and in the lips!

Both sexual tension and food make the mouth water.

How often has a kiss ended up with a little nip, or even a full-fledged bite?

Foods and herbs have been used for centuries to stimulate lovemaking. Now we add to the list—nutritional supplements!

What do you think an aphrodisiac is?

At the broadest level it is *anything* that *excites anybody*. That could mean beautiful women or beautiful men, perfumes, satin sheets, nudity, whippings, body odors, flowers, music, or almost anything you can think of.

If you ask most people what they think an aphrodisiac is, they'll answer that it is something taken internally which improves their sexual relationships. When you're over forty, such "improvement" includes an increase in sexual awareness, both in the genitals and all over the body; achievement of easier, firmer erections; release of inhibitions; prevention of abrupt ejaculations; reversal of sexual deterioration caused by aging; and replenishment of the mind, body, and emotions.

What are these aphrodisiacs? They include restorative foods, herbs, and spices. The judicious use of nutritional supplements can actually manipulate your brain into thinking sexually once again!

All substances that release energy to the body or to the mind can be stimulating, but that stimulation—unless directed to the area of the brain that controls the sexual elements—could just as well have you out washing the car instead of in bed enjoying sex. The substances we seek are those that stimulate the internal hormones governing arousal— that trip the brain's sexual response center.

Our ancestors were seemingly more interested in aphrodisiac stimulation of sexual response than we are; at least, their interest was more out in the open. Maybe TV has dimmed our ardor a bit. However, anybody who has ever made love believes in aphrodisiacs, even if the belief is subliminal.

The poet Ovid recommended honey, pine nuts, eggs, basil, scallions, and rucola.

In *Treasury of Secret Remedies for the Diseases of Women*, a book intended for both men and women, sixteenth century author Jean Liebault discussed the use of nuts, figs, dates, game, fish cooked with onions, chestnuts, spices, and pomegranates.

Dr. Nicolas Venette wrote *Conjugal Love: or the Pleasures of Marriage* in the mid-seventeenth century. His menus included seminal nutrients such as eggs, crabs, prawns, crayfish, beef marrow, and cock's testicles.

Louis XIV and Louis XV added ambergris (no great pleasure to swallow), chocolate, and cloves to the list.

The Doctrine of Signatures, a belief held to this day among certain herbalists, holds that all life on this earth has a relationship. It teaches that the use of a plant or an animal part can be determined by its resemblance to the human organ it can aid.

Therefore, oysters are considered good for the testicles because they *look like testicles*.

This idea appears to be so silly to our "sophisticated" minds that we tend to dismiss the concept out of hand. However, oysters are exceptionally rich in a *concentrated virility food* called zinc! So the theory that connects oysters and sex is not so farfetched after all.

As we investigate "sexy foods" you will see that the scientific community is beginning to confirm what our "ignorant" forbears knew from trial and error.

This is not a diet book; it is a book about virility and food, virility and herbs, virility and nutritional supplements.

Chocolate and Cocoa

Sugar is a forbidden item in diet books, at least if it is used in large quantities, but the first of our sexy foods is bitter chocolate. Bitter chocolate is deep, dark, and delicious. It even smells sexy.

Bitter chocolate contains a stimulating ingredient, the amino acid called phenylethylamine, the same amino acid present in great quantities in the blood stream of people in the first throes of a mad, mad love affair. Frequently, if this love affair results in a "broken heart," the injured party can only be consoled by pounds and pounds of chocolate. Perhaps a chocolate binge replaces the loss of the amino acid that was so pleasurable when it was produced by falling in love.

Bitter chocolate "feels" sexy. It melts on the fingers and begs to be licked off. But chocolate did not start out as the sexy, sweet treat we know. For thousands of years the Indians of Mesoamerica cultivated the tree that bears the cocoa bean. A bitter brew was prepared from the beans. It was considered then to be both nutritious and sexually stimulating, in spite of its bitter taste.

Cocoa was habit-forming even then, before the Spaniards arrived and conquered the Aztec Empire.

Montezuma was addicted to a concoction of cocoa, vanilla, and honey, cooled with snow from nearby mountains. He said the drink helped keep up his virility for the arduous and pleasurable task of satisfying his numerous wives and concubines.

Cocoa was brought back to Europe as an aphrodisiac, but did not become a rage until the discovery of refined sugar. Before then it was considered too bitter to drink. Once the mixture of cocoa and sugar became known, it spread like wildfire. *It became so popular as an aphrodisiac that cocoa was condemned from the pulpit!*

Chocolate's reputation may be well deserved because it has sex-stimulating qualities.

Chocolate contains sugar, which provides energy in its most rapidly usable form. It also contains theobromine, a substance similar in action to caffeine. Chocolate can

- increase digestive secretions
- dilate the bronchioles
- dilate the blood vessels, promoting the flow of blood to the penis
- stimulate the nervous system

A cup of hot cocoa contains about one hundred fifty to two hundred milligrams of theobromine, but a chocolate bar contains very little and is virtually useless for sexual stimulant purposes.

Milk chocolate does not contain enough stimulant because it has been diluted with milk solids and sucrose.

Try Montezuma's cocoa formula, using dark, rich cocoa without milk solids. Milk contains tryptophan, an amino acid that can relax you and prepare you for sleep, not for sexual combat!

Using cocoa with milk at bedtime will help you sleep better, not make love better.

However, using cocoa with hot water, honey, and vanilla will arm you for love's labors.

Cocoa contains important minerals such as calcium, iron, and phosphorus. It is especially rich in phosphorus, a mineral that effects the male erection.

The sexual stimulation of cocoa results from the alkaloid theobromine, the mineral phosphorus, and the particularly sexy taste cocoa leaves in the mouth. Finishing a meal with a stimulating cocoa drink or having a glass before bedtime can help to create the proper combination of *concentrated virility foods* to relieve anxiety and promote the desire for physical contact.

For added fortification, float a chunk of bitter chocolate on the top of your steaming cocoa and feel your saliva and other juices begin to flow.

Don't settle for milk chocolate. Look for a candy store that sells bitter chocolate, the darker and richer the better. Don't stint on the price. A strong erection is worth an extra buck or two! Buy it in chunk style and, when the cocoa is steaming, lower a large piece onto the liquid so that it floats. The first taste on your lips will be creamy, melting dark chocolate, followed by the bitter bite of cocoa, then the smooth caress of honey.

Make sure your wife is nearby drinking the same concoction.

Montezuma used his cocoa fortification nightly and sired many children until the Spanish ended his forays with a silken cord. Since you do not have to worry about the Spanish invading your home, there should be nothing to prevent your excursion into Montezuma's area as often as you like.

Eggs

You've eaten eggs all of your life and never knew how to turn them into sexual stimulants!

There has been so much bad publicity about eating eggs that people have almost given up on one of the best sexy foods we can find.

Doctors have been advising people to give up eggs because they contain cholesterol. They think cholesterol is the cause of some cardiac problems.

But, that may not be so!

Many nutritionists believe that cholesterol has been getting bad publicity. They think that accumulations of cholesterol on the walls of arteries begins *only after a deficiency of one or more nutrients other than cholesterol has damaged the cell wall surface.* Blaming eggs is like blaming a wooden house for the fire caused by a short in the electric wires.

The body needs cholesterol. If it doesn't get it from the diet, it will manufacture it!

Eggs contain about seven grams of high-quality protein and all of the essential amino acids, the ones our bodies cannot make but must obtain from our diet. And, these nutrients are in the exact proportion our bodies need for quick assimilation and body repair.

Eggs are rich in vitamin A and, outside of fish and fish oil, are one of the few foods which contain vitamin D. Vitamin A helps to keep the mucous membrane soft and supple and well lubricated. Eggs also contain vitamin E and some of the B-complex vitamins, particularly pantothenic acid. Pantothenic acid works with the adrenal glands to provide excitement and response to sexual advances.

Eggs are rich in minerals, including calcium, iron, potassium, and sexy phosphorus. They also contain lecithin, one of the raw materials that influences the brain to manufacture sex chemicals. Without the stimulating effect of these sex chemicals, the body cannot react.

How should you prepare eggs for better sex value?

Get fresh eggs, the fresher the better! Read the date on the carton.

Use large eggs and separate the yolk from the white.

Eat the yolk raw. The enzymes and vitamins, the *concentrated virility foods*, are damaged by heat. Any temperature above 98.6 degrees Fahrenheit (body temperature) destroys the sex values found in the yolk.

On the other hand, egg white must be cooked. It contains an enzyme called avidin that binds to one of the important B vitamins, biotin, and prevents it from being absorbed by the body. Once the egg white is heated, the enzyme is inactivated and the biotin is available.

Raw egg yolk may be mixed into tomato juice or V-8, with a squeeze of lemon added for additional taste. Or it can be spread on a cracker with a drop of soy sauce or mixed with raw, chopped onion and served on toast.

Egg white can be fried in a little butter or laid onto boiling water. It can be mixed into a meat loaf recipe before baking, but it must not be eaten raw!

In a book entitled, *The Perfumed Garden for the Soul's Delectation* (and I'm sure you know where the garden exists), a task was set for the hero's friend and companion before the queen would yield her favors to the hero. The test was to stoke her lady in waiting's fire as many times as she desired for fifty days and fifty nights.

The companion agreed to the task set before him, asking only one condition: That he could choose his own diet.

He asked only for raw eggs and bread.

He enjoyed his "stoking" so much that he threw in an extra ten days just for the fun of it!

The use of eggs to increase sexual prowess and to restore sexual vigor is not new, only the preparation is new! And now you know about it also.

A few warnings about eggs: Watch out for cracked eggs. When

eggs are intact they are bacteria-proof; but, if they are cracked, bacteria just love to get in and multiply. Since you will be eating the yolk raw, make sure the egg is fresh and perfect.

Remember, too, that smoking and eggs cannot exist in any type of a sexual union. The poisons in smoke contribute to the loss of the *concentrated virility food* zinc and can lead to an increase in the blood cholesterol level. Zinc is the main mineral found in the prostate gland and in the seminal fluid. You can't have it both ways. You can't contribute to your sex snacks by eating raw egg yolk, and at the same time, create a climate that reduces your erectile ability. So, throw away the cigarettes and say hello to your wife again!

Honey

Warm, sticky, wet, and sweet

This is an apt description of one of the better-known substances often cited for its nutritional and aphrodisiacal quality.

The substance is honey!

Think of the married couple's first nights together. It's called a *honeymoon.*

Honey is made from flower nectar, predigested in the bee's stomach so that the sucrose becomes fructose (*an essential part of male semen*).

Fructose is converted to glucose and burned for energy without the need for waste of digestive energy. Although it does not stimulate a flow of insulin, there is no truth to the fable that it is entirely safe for diabetics. It is, however, about half as harmful as refined white sugar.

Honey is the fastest, safest, most easily absorbed food the body can draw on for sexual energy. In Morocco, as in many other countries, a wedding celebration consists of a feast with honey cakes and a beverage made of honey ale. *The easily absorbed sugar is essential to a quick replenishment of semen, so you can do it again!*

In *The Perfumed Garden*, the author recommends a precoital meal of twenty almonds, one hundred pine nuts, and a glass of honey!

Why this menu?

Almonds contain protein, linoleic acid, iron, calcium, potassium, vitamins B1, B2, and B3, and are loaded with phosphorus.

Pine nuts contain protein, calcium, potassium, vitamins B1, B2, and B3, and a load of phosphorus.

Honey contains all of the energy needed plus aspartic acid for increased stamina, vitamins B1, B2, B3, B6, biotin, pantothenic acid, potassium, sulfur, calcium, sodium, phosphorus, magnesium, silicon, iron, manganese, and copper.

Considering that *The Perfumed Garden* was written in the 1600s, before modern analysis of elements, the author really was aware of the value of *concentrated virility foods*.

Athletes lick a teaspoonful of honey before competing in an event. The quick surge of energy from honey enables them to reach heights they couldn't reach without the additional "push." You can do the same before your next sexual event and count on the energy flow to carry you along with it.

Honey also is an aid to calcium absorption and helps to improve the hemoglobin content of the blood. Hemoglobin is the material that makes blood red. It is involved in carrying oxygen to the muscles and organs of the body. Extra oxygen means more muscle tone and coordination for any activity.

The darker the honey, the more nutrients it contains. Many manufacturers heat honey so it will flow into jars more easily on the production line. The label will not show that the honey has been heated, because the FDA says it can be heated to 160 degrees and still say "uncooked" on the label. But a heat that high destroys the enzymes and a lot of the *concentrated virility foods* it should contain.

Honey is also an anti-lubricant. If more friction is desired, try a honey coating before beginning. The possibilities are endless!

Pressure exerted on the penis during vaginal contact is an

exciting and necessary adjunct to orgasm. Frequently, in older women, the elasticity and tight fit so enjoyable in earlier times has given way to a looser, less satisfying contact. When this situation has arisen, the anti-lubrication quality of honey is desirable.

And, if that is not enough to recommend honey as one of the sexiest of the *concentrated virility foods*, consider how honey can enhance the job of mouth-to-organ contact!

Bee Pollen

Along with honey, one of the world's most perfect foods is bee pollen, sometimes called beebread. It contains all twenty-two of the known elements that compose the human body. Ounce for ounce, it is higher in protein content than meat or eggs, and its amino acid ratio is better than that of any other food.

Pollen is loaded with nutrients.

According to *Analysis of Pollen*, Vivino and Palmer, University of Minnesota, 1944, one gram of bee pollen contains the following:

Vitamin B1	9.2 mg
B2	18.5 mg
B3	200.0 mg
B5	35.0 mg
B6	5.0 mg

It also contains vitamins A, C, and E, as well as potassium, magnesium, calcium, phosphorus, sulfur, iron, manganese, and copper. It contains the bioflavonoid rutin, which strengthens capillary walls and helps to steady the heart's rhythm.

One teaspoon of pollen equals about one thousand pollen pellets.

This is about the daily recommended dose of this *concentrated virility food*.

According to Weygand and Hoffman, 1950, the vitamin C content in one gram of pollen is considered to be small (about seven to fifteen milligrams), depending on the flowers from which the pollen was obtained. However, in combination with the other ingredients, the synergistic action is refreshing.

Human hormones and plant hormones are similar in action.

The sex organ stimulating hormones of plants are similar to the human hormones secreted by the pituitary gland.

In fact, pollen from the date palm contains a hormone that corresponds exactly to human gonadotropin.

The ancient Bedouins of the desert knew this and used the date palm to combat sterility. It is truly amazing that a people without modern training in nutrition knew secrets of *concentrated virility foods* that we are just discovering now!

Doctors in Sweden at the University of Lund and Doctor Ask-Upmark of Uppsala use an extract of pollen called cerniton to treat prostatitis.

A pollen regimen, painless and inexpensive, can restore health, vigor, and dynamism. One teaspoon is enough. Try it for ten days or so as an experiment. If your system's reactions and sexual behavior improve, if your mental and body activities improve, then continue to take it daily.

Royal jelly is not only for the queen bee.

Royal jelly can make you feel like a king. Originally intended for the queen bee, it is thin and milky, two-thirds protein, loaded with B-complex vitamins, C, and D, plus a natural antibiotic. It is a rich source of pantothenic acid and contains a special enzyme that stimulates a high absorption of this amazing vitamin.

We need the power of pantothenic acid to stimulate our adrenal glands.

In humans, pantothenic acid, along with vitamin C, is indispensable to the activity of the adrenal glands. The two nutrients provide the adrenal glands with the energy needed both to combat daily stress and to engage in nightly sex.

Royal jelly has been a factor in increasing the lifespan of lab animals.

In animal experiments, pantothenic acid, the main ingredient in royal jelly, has increased the life span of mice by nineteen percent.

Royal jelly capsules are available in health food stores. Try taking one capsule twice a day between meals. Fresh jelly in capsules is a better source than powdered royal jelly.

What is sexual impotence?

Sexual impotence in men is more frequent than is generally thought. Impotence is usually understood to be the inability to carry out sexual intercourse. However, studies at the Gynecological Clinic at the University of Sarajevo, Yugoslavia, have extended the definition to include poor sperm production.

Although the estimate of a man's potency is usually based on his ability to carry out the sex act, fertilization is another important part of the potency concept.

A lack of potency can be either physical or psychological.

Because pollen is nature's own propagator of life, it is not difficult to understand its role in enhancing the sexual life.

This *concentrated virility food* contains predigested sugars that can be quickly converted into glycogen.

Glycogen is a substance vital to the production of sperm. It contains aspartic acid to help rejuvenate the sex glands. It has also been used as a treatment for sexual lethargy.

Pollen contains serine, a plant hormone similar to gonadotropin.

Gonadotropins cause the testicles to manufacture more of the male hormone testosterone, which acts as a stimulant to all sexual activity.

You may not be interested in having any more children, but it's fun to keep the delivery system in good working order!

Bee pollen is one of the *concentrated virility foods* that can provide raw material for your hungry sex system. Also use extra vitamin C, A, zinc, selenium, and the B-complex vitamins.

Along with a basic vitamin and mineral tablet, daily quanities of nutrients should include:

Vitamin A	up to 20,000 IU a day
Vitamin C	up to 2,000 mg a day
Zinc	up to 50 mg a day
Selenium	up to 200 mcg a day
B complex	up to 50 mg a day

Active sperm in semen is in a mixture of vitamin C, citric acid, phosphorous, ergothioneine, prostaglandin, vesiglandin, adrenaline, noradrenaline, potassium, glyceryl-phosphoryl-choline, and fructose.

Sperm is ninety-five percent concentrated protein, but contains only two calories per teaspoon.

That kind of concentrated power needs *concentrated virility foods*!

Lecithin

Lecithin plus vitamin B1 helps in the production of acetylcholine, which acts as an aphrodisiac for aging brains.

Lecithin breaks down cholesterol into tiny particles. If there is not enough lecithin in the body, cholesterol particles remain too large to leave the blood stream and can become trapped between arterial walls.

The liver can manufacture lecithin if you eat a healthy diet and get enough vitamins and minerals.

If you suspect you are not getting enough naturally, you can buy it in the health food store and supplement your diet!

Lecithin is a concentrated virility food.

It contributes to the production of the adrenal hormones which respond to sexual excitement!

Lecithin improves circulation by helping to clear the blood stream of excess, clogging cholesterol. The better the flow of blood, the better it flows to the penis. It is this flow of blood that causes an erection. Poor circulation can result in a weak erection.

Lecithin is found in all the tissues. It is a special combination of choline, inositol, fats, and essential fatty acids. It helps the body use cholesterol in the manufacture of the *important sex hormones, aldosterone and testosterone.* A lack of lecithin can result in a deficiency of these hormones. Without this important *concentrated virility food,* the male libido slackens and the result is a weak or absent erection!

Sex begins in the brain.

People always say that sex starts in the brain and works its way down to the genitals.

It happens to be true, but not the way most people mean. In order for a person to feel "sexy," the brain must manufacture certain chemicals. These chemicals "instruct" the sex organs to react. One of the most important of these brain chemicals is acetylcholine. If it is not present there are no sexy thoughts, no lubrication to make body parts nice and slippery, perhaps not even the memory of why you're chasing your partner around the room!

Acetylcholine is manufactured from foods in the diet, principally from seafood, but it can also be obtained in quantity from supplemental lecithin offered in health food stores. It is available as a powder, in flake form, in tablets, and in capsules. It can be added to food, sprinkled on salads, or swallowed.

Capsules contain twelve hundred milligrams of lecithin. Two capsules three times a day with meals can really help your body manufacture the acetylcholine it needs under normal circumstances.

Some people need more.

The strength of lecithin depends upon the content of a substance called phosphatidylcholine. The more of this substance present, the stronger the lecithin is. Now, because it has been recognized as a *concentrated virility food*, tablets of phosphatidylcholine are showing up in the market place. One tablet with meals can do wonders for your sex life.

Do not make the mistake of trying to take the powder, the flakes, or even the liquid straight from the bottle. You won't like the taste or the greasy feel. If you use these forms, mix them with food.

Lecithin makes up the protective sheath around sensitive nerve cells.

It can have a calming effect on people who are deficient in this material.

It helps manufacture testosterone, the male sex hormone.

With vitamin B1, it helps the brain think "sexy."

It breaks down cholesterol to lower cholesterol level in the blood.

It contributes to the production of the adrenal hormones so you can react to sexual contact.

It is a crucial component of semen, and helps keep the prostate healthy.

Lecithin is a rich source of phosphorus, the *concentrated virility food* with a direct action on the male sex organ.

It helps to clear the circulation for the unimpeded passage of blood throughout the body. Science has shown that men with circulatory problems have difficulty achieving and sustaining an erection. Your doctor may recommend a dose of lecithin that is higher than that recommended in this chapter.

Meat...Of Meat and Men

Recently, scientists from Emory University published a report on the diet eaten by the early caveman. It seems his diet contained as much as fifty percent meat, supplemented by roots, nuts, and seeds. The meat he ate was much, much lower in fat than the meat we buy today. He must have thrived on the low-fat meat diet, however, because we're here today!

Meat is a source of all the essential amino acids. It is a complete protein, but, men over forty have less acid in their stomachs and, without a plentiful supply of stomach acid, meat is difficult to digest. So it sits, and drives all other thoughts from the mind except one message from the brain: "How are we going to digest it?"

Steaks and chops, the usual favorites of men, are not the favorites of *virile* men. They are more a source of indigestion than of lovemaking!

Organ meats are another story.

Liver and kidneys are a rich source of *concentrated virility foods* including vitamin A, the entire B-complex family, and phosphorus.

The thymus gland (sweetbread), seat of the immune system, and brains are sought after in sexually inclined circles, for these are very rich in natural lecithin, protein, vitamins, and minerals.

Animals don't read books, but they know how to eat. Meat-eating animals leave the steaks and muscle meats behind and eat only the stomach and attached glands. The rest they leave to scavengers.

Animal genitals serve the animal well in life. They can serve humans just as well once they have been removed and prepared for the table.

They have been fed to those who need help with a diminished libido. Cooked testicles of bulls, rams, or goats have graced many a table, as have the testicles of calves.

There is a sexual center in the brain that is aroused when saturated by an excess of sex hormones.

The male gonads consist of canals called seminal tubes and cells which produce hormones—male sex hormones. The hormone testosterone passes directly into the blood stream and influences the organism strongly in the direction of physical and psychological masculinity.

The sexual center of the brain, stimulated by the hormone, projects desire. Appropriate satisfaction eases the hunger, and the center "rests" for an interval.

An excess of male hormone may result in involuntary erections.

Some people are turned off by the idea of a meal with animal procreative parts as the main course. This does not mean that they cannot fortify their parts with the testicular power of the glands.

Gland extracts are more effective for sexual problems than the gland itself!

Protomorphogens, glandular extracts prepared in tablet or capsule form, have often been prescribed to prop up a sagging sex life.

Every function of the body is affected by small amounts of chemical messengers (hormones) which are made in the cells of glands and distributed via the blood stream in tiny amounts that cause an action or reaction.

Raw tissue concentrates, called glandulars or protomorphogens, have been used as *concentrated virility foods* for centuries. Although "raw" really meant uncooked in days gone by (an early treatment for failing eyesight was raw liver soaked in honey), when the term is used today it means that when the gland is processed, the temperature is never allowed to rise above 37 degrees Celsius (98.6 degrees Fahrenheit). This is body temperature, and it is at this temperature that enzymes have their highest degree of activity. Normal cooking temperatures go much, much higher and destroy enzymes, so cooked food will lack the stimulating factors you can get by taking the correctly prepared raw glandulars.

It is for this reason that there is a difference of opinion between those who claim that glandular extracts are more effective for sexual problems than the gland itself once it has been cooked and those who swear by a good meal of gonads!

The proponents of raw glandulars claim that once the glandular material has been cooked it is dead, since its hormonal and enzymatic properties have been lost.

Raw glandulars are available at most health food stores and should be taken along with minerals, vitamins, and selected herbs.

The following combination has been said to be particularly effective:

- Glandulars — "raw" orchic, prostate, pituitary, hypothalamus.
- Vitamins — A, C, D, E, B complex with extra B1 and B2, biotin, PABA, and folic acid.
- Unsaturated fatty acids — either in capsules or use sunflower, safflower, or olive oil on a fresh green salad with apple cider vinegar.
- Minerals — selenium, zinc, manganese, calcium, magnesium, potassium.
- Herbs — pumpkin seeds, saffron, sarsaparilla, damiana.

The combination of raw glandulars can be purchased from health food stores exactly as shown here, or separate raw glandulars are also available if you want to experiment with different com-binations. Do not take them with meals. Wait at least two hours after eating or, take them at bedtime.

Once your energy has been restored and you are again enjoying sexual encounters, slowly wean away from the use of these *concentrated virility foods*. You don't want your own glands to become so dependent on them that they become lazy.

For the vitamins and minerals mentioned, look for a high-potency formula that contains all of the mentioned nutrients plus other vitamins and minerals. Take your multi-vitamin and mineral tablet or capsule twice a day with meals.

Pumpkin seeds should be purchased fresh. Eat a handful every day. If you can find pumpkin seed oil in capsule form, buy a bottle and take one capsule daily along with the fresh seeds. Not only will your sex life flourish but your prostate may never bother you!

Use saffron when you cook brown rice and have that dish at least three times a week.

Once a week, drinking a tea made from sarsaparilla and a tea made from damiana will keep the fire burning in your mind and your genitals.

Detracters of glandular therapy say that glandulars are protein in nature and would be digested in the stomach and can't be expected to influence the organ system.

However, according to studies of nucleic acid metabolism in rats by use of carbon 14-labelled purine and pyrimidine bases and nucleic acids, and H. Greife and S. Molnar, *Anabolic pathways of nucleic acid acid derivatives*, Inst. Tierphysiol. Tierenaehr. Univ. Goettingen, Goettingen, Germany, the glandular substance does migrate to the corresponding gland once it is in the body.

In these studies scientists tagged the carbon molecules in glandulars and let them go into the digestive system. Later, the *tagged molecules* were *found* in the *corresponding gland* of the consuming animal.

In other words, raw glandulars from the sex glands of potent animals, when ingested, can find their way to the corresponding gland in humans.

Therefore, it is a matter of the quality and quantity of available nutrients for any particular gland or tissue. If they are introduced into the body and are available in the blood stream qualitatively and quantitatively, the responding tissue or gland may build, rebuild, or repair itself more readily.

If you are having difficulty because there is not enough hormone being manufactured to act as a stimulus to the sexual center in the brain, the use of these *concentrated virility foods* in the form of raw glandulars prepared from fresh, potent organs of animals in their prime may stimulate your own sex organs into the kind of "ready-to-go-all-night" performance that they gave you in your youth.

Milk—Mother's and Others

Nursing is our first quasi-sexual experience unless we have been forced into an affair with a plastic nipple and milk bottle.

Milk is a sexually fortifying food, and, when mixed with honey, can do wonders for a sagging love life!

Milk is the best natural source of calcium and vitamin B2. Without calcium, muscles cannot contract properly and will cramp. Vitamin D must be present for calcium to be absorbed from the digestive tract. Since milk is fortified with vitamin D, the calcium it contains is made available to the body.

If milk-drinking is continued from childhood on, the body should continue to produce the enzyme necessary to digest it. Many people, however, lose the ability to digest milk and cannot take advantage of the formidable food factors it contains. This comes about because the enzyme called lactase, which is needed to digest the milk sugar (lactose) is no longer produced in the amounts needed. The result is gas, stomach discomfort, and diarrhea. The condition is known as *lactose intolerance* and may be a genetic lack. Chances are, if your parents and grandparents had problems with drinking milk, so will you.

It is possible that you may be able to digest raw cow's milk or goat's milk if you sip it slowly and not with any other foods. Or, you may be able to digest yogurt without having problems.

According to the *Kama Sutra* of Vatsyayana (Burton Version):

"Now the means of increasing sexual vigor are as follows: (a) A man obtains sexual vigor by drinking milk mixed with sugar, the piper chaba (pepper), and licorice. (b) Drinking milk with sugar, and having the testicle of a ram or goat boiled in it, is also productive of vigor." (*Note: The effect can be duplicated by using glandulars if testicles of a ram or goat are difficult to obtain. Raw glandulars appear to have more concentrated virility power than the whole testicle.*) "(c) In the same way if a man mixes with rice the eggs of a sparrow, and having boiled this with milk, adds to it ghee (clarified butter) and honey, and drinks of it as much as necessary it will have the same effect. (d) If a man takes the husks of the sesame seeds and soaks them with the eggs of sparrows, and then having boiled them with milk, mixed with sugar and ghee and the flour of wheat and beans, he is said to be able to enjoy many women. (e) If ghee, honey, sugar, and licorice in equal quantities, the juice of the fennel plant, and milk are mixed together, this nectar-like composition is said to be holy, and provocative of sexual vigor, a preservative of life, and sweet to the taste."

(*Note: Since sparrows' eggs and hen's eggs differ only in size and not particularly in nutritional content, although it is true that sparrows feed only in the wild, it appears to be permissable to substitute hen's eggs in the above formulas.*)

According to the *Ananga-Ranga* of India:

Cucumber, asparagus, and milk appear frequently in the list of culinary aphrodisiacs. Others cited include honey, beans, sugar, eggs, onions, and garlic.

One recipe for weak erections is as follows: "Take 150 grains of the pith of the Moh tree (Bassia latifolia), pound well with a mortar and mix with the milk of a cow. The patient, no matter what his age, will regain vigor and be able to enjoy 100 women." (The flowers of the Moh tree are very rich in sugar, up to fifty-eight percent fermentable sugar. Honey may be substituted for Moh tree pith.)

The male genitalia can be starved for zinc. Cow's milk is one of the best sources next to seafood. Our American diet is sorely lacking in foods which provide this essential mineral in quantities necessary for good sexual health. Milk can be a *concentrated virility food* according to Dr. Paavo Airola.

In *The Perfumed Garden*, Shaykh Nafzawi drank camel's milk strongly laced with honey as a restorative for love's labors.

Seeds and Nut Fruits

Seeds are like eggs. Everything necessary to make a new life is enclosed in a protective shell. Protein, vitamins, minerals, carbohydrates, oils, enzymes, and growth hormone are included.

While they are primarily intended to produce plant life, the ingredients are easily rearranged in our bodies to suit our own needs.

Plant hormones support human hormone production.

Pumpkin seeds support the prostate gland. A declining prostate gland can be helped to return to normal or near normal by the use of pumpkin seeds and supplemental zinc. The natural *concentrated virility foods* in pumpkin seeds (UFA — unsaturated fatty acids) plus zinc offer the raw materials needed by the body to stimulate this sex-adjunct gland back to normal operation.

Plant seeds are close to fifty percent polyunsaturated oil. They are excellent sources of lecithin (needed to manufacture the sex hormones), vitamin E and the B complex, magnesium, potassium, phosphorus, zinc, manganese, vanadium, and molybdenum.

These substances are necessary for cell respiration, metabolism, and enzymatic activity throughout the body and in the genito-urinary tract.

Zinc is now being accepted by the medical professional as one of the prime materials connected with sexual pursuits. Most nuts contain a large amount of this *concentrated virility food*. Other good sources include milk, seafood, liver, and whole wheat products.

Nuts are most nutritious when eaten raw. Roasting changes their digestibility except for starchy nuts like the chestnut, which must be roasted before eating.

Brazil nuts, pumpkin seeds, and sunflower seeds contain large amounts of sex gland stimulating phosphorus, while sesame seeds contain the most calcium. A diet of leafy green vegetables and mixed nuts can supply most of the minerals needed by the body on a daily basis.

Nuts are also rich in protein, ten to fifteen percent, and have a high percentage of easily digested, energy-yielding fat.

Pistachios, one of the earliest cultivated nuts, are mentioned in the Bible. In Genesis 43:11, Jacob instructs his son, who is on his way to Egypt, to take some choice fruits of the land as presents. A little balm and a little honey, some gum myrrh, and some of the finest pistachio nuts.

Pistachios were the favorite of the Queen of Sheba. During her reign in Assyria, she claimed the entire crop for her own. Only she and favored guests were allowed to eat and enjoy them.

The pistachio tree resembles the apple tree and can grow to twenty feet high.

Cashews, although a relative of the pistachio, are dangerous in the wild. They grow at the end of a stalk in a double shell. Between the inner and outside shell is a black, poisonous oil. If the oil is allowed to come in contact with the skin, it can cause intense pain and the skin will blister and peel off. The cashew tree believes in protecting its seed, but man has found ways of harvesting the delicious nut within.

English walnut trees grow to a height of forty to fifty feet. They were originally found in Persia and transplanted anywhere in the world where they could be grown. In ancient times the walnut was used as a snack to clean teeth since it was thought to prevent tooth decay. The Romans pounded it to a powder and made it into a salve to be smeared on dog bites to prevent infection.

Pecans made space trips with the astronauts. On the way to the first lunar landing, they munched on pecans because these nuts are easily digestible, have no waste, provide energy, and do not spoil easily.

Nuts can be added to a crisp green salad to pep up your energy. Or use your blender to grind up almonds, bananas, and milk. Add a dash of honey and a drop of vanilla (considered to be an aphrodisiac since it contains catecholamines, which stimulate mental and physical sexual potential). Drink this mixture and be confident of your own potency.

Take a package of nuts, raisins, and apricots along to the office for that four o'clock energy drop. You'll be amazed at how good you'll feel when you get home!

Lust and Love From The Sea

All life began in the sea, so it's reasonable to assume that the sea contains all of the elements necessary for good health and good sex.

Hen's eggs supply balanced nutrition; fish eggs stimulate sexual response.

Fish eggs (roe) from any fish are fine, but when we think of caviar we mean the roe from the sturgeon.

What does this fabulous food contain that makes it tops in the sex game?

In one hundred grams of caviar there are three hundred thirty-five milligrams of bioactive phosphorus ready for metabolic activity. The phosphorus is available for human needs since it has been transformed by the sturgeon and combined with other nutrients needed for easy assimilation.

Caviar is the treatment of choice in cases of nutritionally reversible impotence, according to Doctor William J. Robinson in his book, *America's Sex and Marriage Problems.*

Because caviar also contains a rich amount of calcium, it is useful for motor muscle contraction, a necessary body action for intercourse.

Arnold Lorand, M.D., of Carlsbad, wrote *The Increase of Sexual Activity by a Specially Adapted Diet.* In his book he says, "Since the most remote periods of the existence of man, the eating of fish has been accredited with the property of increasing sexual activity. It was for this reason that the old Egyptians forbade the eating of fish by the priests...

"Other articles of diet, particularly eggs and caviar, are also supposed to exert a stimulating action upon sexual activity."

Lorand also states that when the male sex glands are "well-filled" they exert a stimulus upon the sensory sexual centers. About fish and caviar he points out that the phosphorus content may be the chief activating principle. He mentions other phosphorus-containing foods, including truffles (a source, also, of iron), lobster, and crab.

Eels look as though they should have a considerable sexual function because they bear a strong resemblance to the male organ. They do have a rich vitamin A and vitamin D content, higher in potency than any other fish. Vitamin A acts as an antioxidant to protect sensitive sexual tissue from the action of destructive free radicals. Vitamin A is also necessary to keep mucous membrane moist and free of infection.

Eels and shellfish contain a wide variety of needed ingredients including phosphous and zinc in the most bioactive form. They also are a prime source of iodine, which is needed by the thyroid gland to manufacture thyroid hormones. The thyroid gland regulates metabolic activity in the body and a lack of iodine can result in a sluggish thyroid. If the basal metabolic rate (BMR) is low, the whole body reacts in a tired and uninterested manner to all actions including those which involve sex.

Oysters have long been recognized as a sexual stimulant. So, too, have clams, mussels, shrimp, and crabs.

Ovid recommended crabs, all kinds of shellfish, snails, and eggs. Plus pine nuts and honey.

It is said that one of the most powerful of Chinese aphrodisiacs is the celebrated bird's nest soup.

This delicacy is prepared from the nests of the sea-swallow (salangame). When made correctly, it contains an assortment of spices much like those used by the French in preparing crayfish soup. How can a bird's nest be an aphrodisiac? The explanation is simple.

The nests are made from edible seaweed, usually heavily laden with fish spawn. The fish spawn is rich in phosphorus, which has a powerful action, increasing both desire and erection.

An old recipe for those who could not afford all the caviar they wanted was to mix the following:

1   tablespoon anchovy paste
1   tablespoon minced chives
1   tablespoon chopped pimento
½   teaspoon lemon juice

Add an equal amount of caviar. Spread on thin toast, and enjoy the taste and the energy.

It is said that Catherine the Great, when she needed to produce an heir and the union with her husband brought no results, resorted to pounds of caviar and the services of a member of the royal guard. Either or both had the desired effect and an heir was soon conceived.

The Vietnam War exposed many Americans to the poor-man's version of bird's nest soup. It is called *nuoc-man*. It is an extract from rotted fish and its preparation is similar to that of cod liver oil. It tastes like fish oil and contains a fairly high percentage of phosphorus. The flavor is improved by the use of garlic and pimento — additional aphrodisiacs.

A modern recipe using the roe of herring may be interesting to try:

1   tin of soft herring roe
½   ounce of butter
Salt
Flour
Hot toast
Fried potatoes
Tomatoes, sliced

Roll the roe in flour and add to melted butter in a frying pan. Sprinkle lightly with salt. Serve on hot, buttered toast with fried potatoes and sliced tomatoes. Add sliced cucumbers if desired.

Tuna salad with vegetables originated as an erotic food. Mix the following health-giving, taste-pleasing ingredients:

1 can of tuna
Sliced cucumber
Lettuce
Radishes
Tomatoes, sliced
Spanish capers
Grated raw carrots
Mayonnaise to taste

Or try an oyster salad:

1 dozen oysters, shucked or on the half shell
Lettuce
Cooked and sliced beetroot
Olives
Tomatoes
Grated raw carrots
Onions or leeks
Salt and pepper to taste
Lemon juice as needed

Arrange ingredients on a bed of lettuce. Enjoy!

How far will a man go to restore his sexual virility? How about a gamble with death! Supposedly the world's most potent aphrodisiac is the Fugu. It is a species of puffer fish whose flesh, when prepared correctly, is eaten raw as sashimi, and whose testicular fluid is mixed with warmed saki and sipped.

The problem is that while certain parts of the fish are edible, they are intertwined with other areas that contain a deadly, quick-acting nerve poison called tetradoxin. The preparation of Fugu requires the cook to have studied for years and to have passed all examinations as a Fugu chef. Approximately twenty-five percent of all people who study to be a Fugu chef finally get their diplomas.

The poison in Fugu is so virulent that it is said to be the main component of a concoction that makes a zombie of a human being. The merest trace destroys the will and, although the zombie concept was once thought to be only folklore, science has seen living proof.

With all of this evidence, numbers of Japanese and Westerners take their chances anyway. If the cook has made a mistake, the customer will never leave the restaurant, at least not under his own power. He will die in mid-mouthful! There is no known antidote.

What makes the Fugu an accepted aphrodisiac? Is it the thrill of a close call with death? Is it that the poison is diluted through the fish's body so it is attenuated in the edible portion? No one knows, but about three hundred people get the last thrill of their lives every year.

Fruits and Vegetables

Eat your vegetables and you'll grow up to be big and strong and be able to do it in your eighties and nineties.

Vegetables can be very tasty, but not the way they're usually prepared. They often fall onto the plate, limp, messy, with no taste; a glutinous mass of greenish blah.

When you were a child you had little control over your own food. Now you're an adult and can eat anything you want and can prepare it any way that pleases you.

Vegetables are best either raw, lightly cooked, or steamed. In that way, the natural, good taste is preserved and the vitamin and mineral content is not wasted. Buy a steamer for your asparagus and broccoli. You'll eat better and your sex life will be given a natural lift.

Artichokes. This vegetable is actually a form of thistle and a member of the sunflower family. Catherine de Medici used it as her favorite aphrodisiac, feeding the leaves and the choke to suitors, so it is said.
Artichokes contain potassium, calcium, phosphorus, and some of the B vitamins. Steamed and served with a butter sauce, they can be stimulating to the appetite. The choke is the flower head, the actual reproductive organ of the plant, which may be the reason it is thought of as a sexual stimulant.
Artichokes were used to calm the nerves in some areas of the world, and a flour made from them has been used to make low-calorie pasta.

Asparagus. This vegetable was used as a medicine before it was brought to the table as a food. It is a member of the lily family, and in Japan and China is cooked with sugar or candied as a delicacy. Its principle constituents are: vitamin A, vitamin B complex, manganese, iron, phosphorus, asparagine, rutin, and vitamin C.

Rutin helps to heal and strengthen small capillaries, while the asparagine is a stimulant to the kidneys. Asparagus imports a characteristic odor to the urine. The phosphorus helps to make sex hormones.

Although there is some disagreement in scientific circles, asparagus is said to contain quantities of aspartic acid. This amino acid is used in the process of transamination, by which nitrogen from excess protein is eliminated from the body.

The combination of nutrients in asparagus helps to eliminate waste material from the cells, take out free ammonia circulating in the blood (a cause of fatigue), and—due to its diuretic action— serves as a mild stimulant to the sexual organs.

Culpeper claimed that a brew of asparagus roots boiled in wine and taken early in the morning for several days running "stirreth up bodily lust in man or woman."

Madame de Pompadour offered asparagus sticks at her intimate dinners.

The Perfumed Garden says asparagus should be blanched and sauteed. Josephine Baker swore by bananas, but most Parisians followed Rabelais's "uniterminal, intercrural asparagus stalk."

Avocado. This fruit is a powerful source of protein and other wonders. Its principle constituents are: vitamins A and B complex, vitamin E, seventeen minerals, and amino acids including tryptophane, tyrosine, and cystine.

Avocado is a virtually complete food and is easily digested. Its vitamin A is in the form of Beta-carotene, one of the protective vitamins used against a host of ills.

Its amino acid content helps to build neurotransmitters (serotonin, phenylalanine, noradrenaline), which stimulate sex activity.

It also helps to combat urinary infections by increasing the acidity of the urine.

Banana. Bananas provide vitamins A, B complex, C, E, potassium and other minerals.

The banana stabilizes nerve function and helps to increase

energy. It has been said to be helpful in arthritis and its potassium content helps compensate for the loss of body potassium when prescription diuretics are used.

Green Beans. The principle constituents of green beans are: vitamin A, B complex, C, inositol (found mostly in the strings), phosphorus, calcium, copper, cobalt, and chlorophyll.

Green beans help to promote the normal function of the liver and the pancreas and help to stimulate kidney function. They can be put through a juicer and their juice taken daily to aid rheumatism and gout.

A body without pain is more likely to indulge in sex!

Celery. Celery contains vitamins A, B complex, C, magnesium, manganese, iodine, iron, copper, sodium, potassium, calcium, and phosphorus.

Celery is a strong diuretic and is best when eaten with the feathery green leaves intact.

John Lust's *Herb Book* lists the oil distilled from knob celery (celeriac) as a remedy to restore potency after illness.

Madame de Pompadour used the following dish to rekindle the waning ardor of the king. Try it; maybe you'll like it!

> Chop, scald, and drain two celery stalks. Heat celery in a sauce pan with 1 tablespoon of butter. Then add 1 teaspoon of flour, celery stock to cover, and two egg yolks mixed with ½ cup of light cream. Sprinkle with nutmeg and garnish with sliced truffles.

Chard. Chard provides vitamin A, C, and iron.

Swiss chard and tomatoes make a pleasant salad. A broth prepared from a quarter pound of Swiss chard to a quart of water helps to overcome urniary tract inflammation, constipation, hemorrhoids, and skin disease. All of these conditions are deterrents to a happy sex life.

Carrots. Their principle constituents are: vitamin A (Beta-carotene), B complex, C, iron (up to seven percent), phosphorus, calcium, sodium, potassium, magnesium, manganese, sulfur, copper, bromine, asparagin, and daucarin.

To write about carrots would require a book by itself. Eat carrots! Juice carrots and drink the juice plain or mixed with cabbage juice. Make carrot soup or use in salads.

Daucarine is a strong dilator of blood vessels and may be of help in the sexual area.

Eggplant. Its principal constituents are: vitamin A, phosphorus, and calcium.

The natural attributes of eggplant calm anxiety, aid liver and pancreas function, and promote the flow of urine.

Garlic and Onions. It was in the early 1920s when a Russian scientist and biologist, Alexander Gurvich, discovered that onions were radioactive. Not in the same way that uranium is radioactive, but in a growth-stimulating manner. Specifically, he found that if an onion's growing tip was pointed at the growing tissue of another onion, there was a dramatic increase in the rate of growth. Cell division took place at an increased rate.

He named this mysterious ability "mitogenetic radiation," and later found that it existed in garlic and ginseng as well. The concept excited scientists and they tried to duplicate his experiments with varying degrees of success. Eventually, the idea was dropped as being too difficult to pursue, but now there is renewed speculation that what Gurvich discovered was the focus of the onion's energy field.

Whether or not there are life-enhancing rays from onion, garlic, and ginseng root, mankind has considered these plants very beneficial since earliest times. Onion and garlic have been eaten before work, before war, and before lovemaking to give the eater strength for the job.

The earliest strike on record was during the building of the pyramids. The Egyptian laborers walked off the job when the supply of garlic ran out. They didn't return to the task of preparing the tomb until a new supply was rushed in.

Onions and garlic have been used medicinally against high blood pressure, infection, cholesterol, respiratory infection, and skin infections. Modern science is now discovering that the old science was right. Garlic is being used as a medicine today. It is being prescribed for treatment of high blood pressure, two capsules three times a day with meals, and experiments have shown that both garlic and onion juice are effective against asthma. High-cholesterol sufferers are being told to include garlic in their diet or to use garlic capsules.

In early Rome, Martial advised eating onions to remedy an exhausted penis, and Petronius recommended snails and onions as a fortifying dish.

When one of the heroes of *The Perfumed Garden* is required to maintain an erection for thirty days in order to gain the girl of his dreams, he does so by drinking onion juice and honey.

Garlic and onions promote a healthy digestion, killing off unwanted bacteria. They may also help to rid the body of poisonous metals that interfere with all body actions, metals such as mercury, lead, and cadmium.

The sulfur compounds in onions and garlic appear to be the active ingredients, along with potassium and phosphorus.

Legumes. Beans contain protein, calcium, iron, potassium, and phosphorus. When eaten with other plants or with animal protein, they have been a reliable source of amino acids throughout the ages. The soybean is an efficient source of protein by itself and tofu (made from soybean) is a substitute for meat in China and other parts of the world, including the United States.

The concentrated nutrition in lima, navy, black, red, broad, haricot, kidney, and pinto beans can help supply the energy you need for physical love-play.

According to an old recipe, this food is invigorating for those tired souls: Heat one part onion juice with two parts honey until the onion juice is absorbed. Add three parts water. Soak chick peas in this mixture for twenty-four hours and drink some of the liquid before your next amorous exercise.

Mushrooms. Mushrooms are not usually thought of as sex foods, but they do contain potassium, niacin, and phosphorus and appear to be the only vegetable to contain glycogen. Glycogen is the form in which our body stores carbohydrate until it is needed for energy. Mushrooms, garlic, and onions, sauteed in butter and served with eggs, make one of the tastiest dishes to tempt the palate and provide a good source of energy for any act!

Brewer's Yeast

This is a one-celled plant, but, despite its small size, it is a powerhouse food. Brewer's yeast earned its name because it is a by-product of brewing. When grown for human consumption it may be called primary yeast or nutritional yeast. If the label says "debittered" it means that after the yeast has been washed free of beer it has been treated to make it taste better.

Yeast is a good source of protein (as much as fifty percent), and contains the B complex family as well as two important trace minerals, selenium and chromium. These two minerals, notably lacking in highly processed foods, are present in yeast in forms that are safe and bioavailable.

The chromium value of brewer's yeast is ten times greater than that from other good sources such as calf's liver or wheat germ.

Yeast is also high in the sex mineral phosphorus. An easy way to obtain phosphorus is to use a yeast supplement on a daily basis.

Yeast is also rich in nucleic acids including RNA, the cellular component that governs many vital processes, including the rate of aging. Yeast helps the body's glucose tolerance mechanism function properly. This is important in the control of blood sugar. Also, judging from animal experiments, yeast may help to control cholesterol.

Should anyone avoid yeast? Yes! Gout sufferers. Yeast is high in the nucleic acids that form purines.

Desiccated Liver

The excellent values in liver have long been recognized by nutritionists. Liver is an excellent source of many nutrients. However, once again, it is not for gout sufferers.

Desiccated liver is defatted so the product has a long shelf life. Keep the capsules in a cool place, but not in the refrigerator. In capsule form it has most of the nutrients that make liver an important food.

Kelp

Kelp is among many sea plants known as algae. It has been harvested and used traditionally by the Japanese, Chinese, Eskimos, Icelanders, Danes, and Irish.

Kelp contains some protein and carbohydrate values, but its claim to fame is in its rich mineral and trace-mineral content. Kelp picks up all of the minerals in the water in which it grows. It has the ability to retain these minerals and to concentrate them.

It is richest in iodine, copper, iron, and magnesium, but — when analyzed — appears to contain virtually all of the elements from A to Z.

Iodine is present in the same form as is found in the thyroid gland, and therefore is bioavailable. The thyroid governs the rate at which we burn food and the energy available to the body for all activity. Without enough available iodine the body is in no shape to do anything more strenuous than get in and out of bed — to sleep!

Find Your Own
Fountain of Youth

We see people of fifty-five and sixty, or even people in their nineties, who still play tennis, compete in marathons, and put others—years younger than themselves—to shame in a "sack race."

They're vibrant and creative, quick with their minds and their bodies.

They've discovered, as you will, that the fountain of youth begins in the mind and in the brain, and that both the mind and the brain can be influenced by food and food supplements.

Concentrated virility foods in the form of selected amino acids can restore your virility, help your memory, ease your aching back, and put you in a better mood.

First you have to gain some knowledge about how the brain works.

It's like Ma Bell's telephone network, except for one important difference: The wires don't quite touch one another. There's a little space between the end of one wire (nerve cell) and the beginning of another.

So, the signal has to be carried over that space by special messengers.

These messengers are called *neurotransmitters*.

The neurotransmitters carry messages back and forth. They carry instructions that are sent all over the body. These instructions tell us when to eat, when to sleep, when to have an erection, when to make love, when we are not interested. Sometimes the message center can't get the love message across the space because the neurotransmitter has shut down!

There are two brains. The "old" brain and the "new" brain. The old brain served mankind when we were a young species, fighting to survive in a hostile world of caves, saber-toothed tigers, and mastodons.

The old brain (sometimes called the reptile brain) is the area in which our primitive emotions are stored.

It is the seat of sexual drive and aggression.

Without these two drives, mankind would not have survived.

Brain cells communicate with each other at fantastic speed, through the neurotransmitters. As instructions reach certain brain areas, other body areas are activated. When there are many neurotransmitters available, body reaction is swift and reliable. When there are fewer transmitters available, as in an aging person, the phone lines are sometimes "busy" and, in some cases, "out of order."

But that does not mean they are lost forever. They may be only in hiding, waiting for enough of the neurotransmitters to show up and carry their messages once again!

The neurotransmitters associated with primitive drives, such as sex, include norepinephrine, dopamine, acetylcholine, and others with names just as long and just as difficult to pronounce. We need to know little about their names but much about how to get them manufactured and activated.

Neurotransmitters are obtained from food, as are all of the nutrients we need to run our body. But, there's a problem in just counting on food to supply nutrients in the extra quantities we need to overcome the "busy" signal in the brain.

Nature set up a protective barrier around the brain. When mankind was very young, we didn't know too much about edible food and poisonous food. We picked up anything that didn't eat us first and put it in our mouths. The substance eaten was carried to the brain by the blood stream, but it was examined by the brain barrier before it was permitted to enter the brain space. If the barrier thought it was harmful, it was refused entrance. If it was *useful* to the brain, it was ferried across the barrier by special cells.

That selective action by the brain barrier must be controlled by us in order to achieve the actions we want!

Acetylcholine, for example, when present in sufficient quantities, controls the release of a hormone called vasopressin, a memory and learning chemical. If there are low levels of acetylcholine, we are inclined to be forgetful, lack the ability to concentrate, and ignore sex for the most part.

Acetylcholine is part of what is called the cholinergic system, which controls sensory input. Too little acetylcholine and you'll be so distracted by any activity going on in your environment that you won't be able to think, sleep or make love. The cholinergic system also controls normal muscular activity, coordination, and motor response. All these actions are needed for lovemaking.

But there are more activities needed to keep sex action at a proper level: Things that should happen automatically, but don't unless the brain sends a message.

The cholinergic network keeps mucous membrane lubricated and slippery.

If the level of acetylcholine drops too low, the mucous membrane becomes dry, easily irritated, prone to infection and damge. Sex is no fun with raw, irritated tissue that cannot respond in a natural, normal manner.

Neurotransmitters are produced in the body from the food you put on the table. If you put the right foods on the table, you will be able to influence the production of neurotransmitters in the direction you wish to go. At least, a little!

For instance, acetylcholine is made from choline, one of the members of the B-complex family of nutrients.

Fish contains choline.

Therefore, increasing the amount of fish you eat will influence the amount of acetylcholine produced in the brain.

True, but within reason. That "reason" is the normal metabolism of the body.

All substances compete with each other for passage through the brain barier into the brain area.

Choline is just *one* of the substances in food.

The brain barrier decides which substances, and how much of each, will pass at a certain time. Unless the barrier is overwhelmed by the amount of choline present, compared to the amounts of other nutrients present, only a small amount will be permitted to enter.

And this is the clue:

Once you have increased the raw material needed by the brain to produce the neurotransmitters you wish to have present in quantity, you can overwhelm the odds and actually manipulate the brain into doing what you want it to do!

You can improve your sex life at any age.

You can improve your memory.

You can improve your mood.

You can provide the brain with raw material from food, *and tip the dice in your favor and add more of the raw material by taking a concentrated virility food supplement.*

In that way, when the brain barrier chooses the substances it will allow to be ferried across, it will let in more choline because there will be more choline in proportion to the other substances present.

Imagine, you can influence your own brain to produce the chemicals you need for a better sex life.

What is that *concentrated virility food* which will provide a better balance of choline?

It's called lecithin!

Lecithin is made commercially from soybeans and is available at all health food stores and some drug stores. It comes in tablets, capsules, flakes, powder, and liquid.

Lecithin contains about twenty percent phosphatidyl choline, the raw material the brain uses to make its acetylcholine. So, if you take lecithin with meals, you will provide raw material from the meal itself (assuming you are sitting down to a fish dinner) and will add extra raw material from the supplement.

The flakes or ganules can be sprinkled over a green salad, over cereal, or mixed into gravy. Tablets or capsules can be taken with meals or immediately after meals. The usual dose of the capsules (they contain twelve hundred milligrams of lecithin) or tablets is two with each meal. If you prefer the flakes or the powder, take one tablespoonful with meals.

Do not try to take the powder or the flakes, or even the liquid for that matter, straight from the bottle. Lecithin has a slightly soapy taste unless disguised by food.

For even more concentrated virility power, you can look for and find tablets of phosphatidyl choline that have about a seventy percent active ingredient. Some even come with vitamin B1, which has to be present in the body when choline becomes acetylcholine. If you can find these tablets, they can be taken one daily with meals.

Other food beside fish can supply choline to the diet. Beef liver, brewer's yeast, eggs, peanuts, and wheat germ are good sources. So you see that you can balance your diet by choosing meals that supply brain food, and you can add supplemental choline as well.

Since all nutrients work with other nutrients to achieve more power, be sure that other B-complex vitamins are included in your daily intake, particularly B12, folic acid, inositol, and methionine (an amino acid).

Norepinephrine is another of the brain's neurotransmitters important to primitive drives such as sex. It is also important to memory and learning.

If there is an insufficient supply of norepinephrine, people tend to become depressed, and depressed people have a reduced desire for sex. You may not even know the cause, just that you don't feel like making love. The depression doesn't have to be deep enough to bring in a doctor and you might call it "just a mood."

Two amino acids found in health food stores can turn that mood swing into a more sexually productive mood.

The brain uses L-phenylalanine and L-tryosine to manufacture the neurotransmitter norepinephrine.

Both of these amino acids are found in eggs, meat, and cheese. Both are readily available in these foods, but the same problem with the brain barrier exists as with lecithin and acetylcholine.

There must be enough of the raw material circulating around the brain barrier to swing a reaction in your favor.

The best answer is to eat the beneficial menu during the day and take the amino acid at night before you go to bed.

Both L-phenylalanine and L-tyrosine are available in tablets. An effective amount can be from one hundred milligrams to five hundred milligrams at night before bedtime.

Try to take it for two weeks to see the results.

CAUTION: If you suffer from hypertension (high blood pressure), L-phenylalanine can cause a rise in pressure in some individuals. In that case, with your doctor's consent, L-tyrosine can be used.

Also L-phenylalanine should not be used if the condition PKU (phenylketonuria) is present, or if there is pigmented melanoma, a type of cancer.

Finally, none of these recommendations, except those which have to do with foods, should ever be used during pregnancy.

The idea of actually being able to manipulate the manufacture of brain chemicals in our favor is an intriguing one. Getting past the brain barrier with supplements to tilt the emotions in the right direction is one of the answers to sexual dysfunction.

There is another possible reason for this dysfunction that has to do with our particular needs for certain nutrients.

According to Doctor Roger Williams, there are other reasons for using supplements to stimulate emotions. They have to do with individual needs.

There are two conditions that may arise concerning nutrients. One is a condition of a "deficiency," while the other is a condition of "dependency."

They sound alike, but are worlds apart!

If a person is deficient in love-chemicals he can make the situation right by simply adding the right foods to his diet. The body will take the raw material from the food and restore the balance.

But, if a person is *dependent on certain nutrients, it means he was born with a greater need for them than can be satisfied by dietary means* no matter how much food is eaten.

A nutrient-dependent person would have to use supplements to get back into the normal swing of things.

For example, consider the neurotransmitter called serotonin. It needs the amino acid L-tryptophan as raw material for it to be manufacturered in the brain. Foods which contain L-trypophan are lean meat, poultry, fish, and peanuts. Potatoes and pasta also supply a good quantity of it.

But, there are twenty amino acids in the food and they all want to get into the brain area, so even if you eat meat and pasta or turkey and potatoes, there's no guarantee that more than a small amount of L-tryptophan will reach the brain.

Serotonin is one of the brain chemicals that influences anxiety and is the main chemical involved in helping you to get a good night's sleep.

Anxiety and sleeplessness contribute to the decline and fall of the male organ!

Sleep disorders are common as people age. There is increasing difficulty in falling asleep and sleeping comfortably through the night. Irritability is a common side effect of sleeplessness, so the inner production of serotonin can contribute to a good night's sleep and enjoyable sex before you sleep.

What to do?

First try food! A banana and a glass of milk at bedtime. Both contain L-tryptophan in small quantities and may be all of the raw material you need if you are merely deficient in this amino acid.

If that doesn't work, then you may have to resort to a supplement tablet of L-tryptophan.

Your local health food store or drugstore will have these tablets in five hundred milligram doses. Try taking one tablet at night or even two if necessary. Since vitamins are necessary for the nutritive production line, particularly vitamin B6, you may want to make sure you take a multivitamin during the day and an extra small amount of B6 along with your L-tryptophan tablet. Twenty-five milligrams of B6 should be sufficient.

There may be some additional benefits that help your love life as well. Because L-tryptophan is a smooth-muscle relaxant, it may relieve headaches that interfere with physical communication.

There are other neurotransmitters that contribute to sex. One of them is called dopamine. It influences how you move (locomotion), how you feel about sex, and whether or not you're in the mood!

Dopamine and norepinephrine, although separate brain chemicals, are closely related. The dopaminergic system appears to decline rapidly in the aging brain, calling for either a stimulation of the system or an increase in norepinephrine, since each can be converted into the other.

Dopamine and norepinephrine are called catecholamines. They are deeply involved in sexual behavior and aggression. If there is a low level of these chemicals, there can be a loss of motivation, causing a person to become apathetic and not care about living anymore. If you don't care about living, you certainly don't care about sex!

CAUTION: Before you assume that declining functions are due to your age, consult your doctor to make sure that you don't have anemia, diabetes, or some such condition that may be interfering with your sexual ability.

Also: Do not take any of the amino acids, particularly L-phenylalanine or L-tyrosine if you're taking monamine oxidase inhibitors (MAOI) that have been prescribed by your doctor. If you do, you can have a nasty reaction.

By the way, choline, lecithin, and other brain chemicals, which may be obtained from the diet or from supplements, rarely stimulate sexual action in younger people, but commonly affect people over forty, so this book is not for kids!

The catecholamines mentioned in the previous paragraphs are also involved in the regulation of the release of an aphrodisiac polypeptide hormone called luteinizing hormone-releasing hormone (LHRH) from the hypothalamus, a master gland in the brain. Nature tries to insure the life of the species, so a provision is made within the brain's chemistry to make men horny and women attractive to them. It's natural, it's wonderful, and it's plain fun to be sexy!

A depressed sexual drive in middle or later years may be due to an excess of a hormone called prolactin. About twenty percent of male problems are due to this negative hormone. You cannot diagnose this condition for yourself, but your doctor can run some clinical tests and get the answer. If it should turn out to be so, another amino acid, gamma-aminobutyric acid (GABA), has been known to be effective in most cases.

We will go into the use of vitamins and the part they play in sexual performance later on in this book. However, it has been discovered that certain cells and tissues in the sexually responsive areas are very sensitive to damage from "free radicals" from within and without the body. To protect those areas and insure the best reactions, some antioxidant vitamins and minerals should be taken on a daily basis.

They are vitamins A, E, C, the minerals zinc and selenium, and the amino acid L-cysteine. Also, the B-complex family of vitamins is necessary in the conversion of food to neurotransmitters. Make sure that your daily vitamin contains all of the mentioned nutrients.

Concentrated Virility Foods— Amino Acids Reference Chart

Amino Acid	Influence	Quantity	When Taken
Lecithin	Production of acetylcholine Memory Sex drive Lubrication Coordination	1 tablespoon or 2 capsules 1200 mg each	With meals
Phosphatidyl-choline	Same as above	1 tablet 500 mg	With meals
L-Phenylalanine	Production of noradrenaline Aggression Sex drive Mood for the better	1 tablet 500 mg	At bedtime
L-Tyrosine	Same as above but to be used if blood pressure is high		
L-Trypophan	Anxiety 500 mg	250 to	During the day
L-Tryptophan	Sleeplessness 1,000 mg	500 to	At bedtime
Vitamin B6	Adjunctive influence on all of above	50 mg	Twice a day
Niacinimide	Adjunctive influence on all of above	50 mg	Once a day

Oh, my aching back! It interferes with gardening, walking, and lovemaking!

And nobody offers any help. The doctor says it's your age, and you should learn to live with it.

No way!

Not when there are easy answers waiting on the shelf of your health food store or drug store, and no prescription required.

The answer may be discovered in a combination of amino acids that has been found to be effective in relieving low back pain in many cases.

It's called D-phenylalanine. It's similar to the L-phenylalanine that stimulates the neurotransmitters, but it's also different. Here's how it differs: L-phenylalanine is found in nature while D phenylalanine is made in the laboratory.

They're cousins.

But they act in a different manner when they're combined on a fifty-fifty basis. In combination, they help the body's pain-killers to work longer and better, particularly on low back pain. They do not have side effects like aspirin and, if you have to use aspirin, you can cut the dose in half and take the amino acid tablets with it.

It's not harmful.

It's not habit forming.

The effects increase with time, and you can't "overdose" on it.

It helps to combat the depression that goes along with chronic pain.

You can't separate emotions from physical pain. If we are in pain, we don't think about anything else. Irritability and depression chase all other thoughts out of the mind. If chronic pain can be alleviated easily without using a drug that depresses the central nervous system (like codeine or morphine), it pays to give it a try.

Capsules or tablets are available in either three hundred seventy-five milligram or five hundred milligram doses.

Results vary from person to person, depending on a variety of factors.

Take two tablets or capsules fifteen to thirty minutes before meals for a total of six daily.

Continue to take them until relief is felt. Once there is pain relief, begin to reduce the dosage, but use it throughout the day as before.

Usually, after two months of usage, the tablets or capsules can be taken only one week each month and there will still be pain relief.

Do you chase your wife around the room, but then forget why?

In the natural aging sequence, your mental functions can decline along with other body functions, or they can remain sharp and facile. Nutrition plays an important role in whether or not your brain will remain in top form.

Although much remains to be learned about the chemistry of memory, some of the factors are understood.

RNA synthesis is necessary for memory.

Vitamin B12 stimulates the production of RNA in the brain.

Choline and lecithin supply the raw material for the production of acetylcholine, a stimulant to memory.

Calcium pantothenate or pantothenic acid (vitamin B5) helps in the conversion of choline to acetylcholine.

Phenylalanine is used by the brain to make noradrenaline, and vitamin C and pyridoxine (B6) help produce it. Noradrenaline makes it easier to concentrate and remember.

Vitamin A, B1, E, zinc, and selenium are also needed.

So you see, all of the nutrients mentioned work together to make you feel younger than you are; help you to increase your energy level in work, sports, or sex; and help you improve your intimate relations with your wife or girlfriend!

All things are possible with *concentrated virility foods.*

Herbs and Stimulants

Stimulants can make people feel more alert and energetic by activating or exciting the nervous system. Some stimulants are plants found in nature, and some are amino acids derived from foods and used in a special, concentrated form.

The individual nerves in our bodies communicate with each other electrically and chemically. A nerve impulse is an electrical discharge that moves along the fiber of a nerve cell. The fiber may end at a muscle, a gland, or another nerve cell, but there is always a tiny space between the end of one nerve cell and the beginning of another cell. To bridge the gap and be able to send the message, the nerve cell releases a neurotransmitter, a powerful chemical that affects the abutting cell. Some neurotransmitters are stimulants that cause muscle cells to contract, gland cells to secrete, or other nerve cells to electrically discharge.

One of the common neurotransmitters is called noradrenaline or norepinephrine. It is chemically related to the hormone adrenaline or epinephrine, which is produced by the adrenal glands. Stimulants cause nerve fibers to release noradrenaline and other stimulating neurotransmitters. So, the reaction people feel when they take a stimulating herb or certain amino acids is the result of their own body's chemical energy going to work in the nervous system!

The release of chemical energy in the form of noradrenaline causes predictable changes in both the mind and body. It makes a person feel wakeful, alert, and often happy. The heart beats faster, and there may be a rise in blood pressure. It also may cause butterflies in the stomach and possibly a case of diarrhea.

Stimulants may supress hunger, may make it possible to concentrate better and be more alert to situations and surroundings. The reason the stimulants may supress hunger probably is that they are preparing the body for an emergency. If there is an emergency, all digestive functions become nonessential, and energy is shifted from the intestines to the brain, heart, and blood vessels.

Stimulants sound attractive, but one of life's basic rules is that you don't get something for nothing. After the "up" comes the "down." Unless you're using amino acids, the price you pay for feeling good may be to feel bad!

Coffee and Other Caffeine-Containing Plants

Caffeine, the most popular natural stimulant, is found in a number of plants throughout the world. It was first isolated from coffee in 1821, and was named for the coffee plant. The coffee tree is native to Ethiopia, but is cultivated in many tropical countries throughout the world.

According to legend, nomads found that their flocks became too frisky to sleep after feasting on the fruit of certain trees. Eventually they learned to roast the beans and prepare a drink from them and the first coffee habit was born.

Because coffee is so universally accepted as a beverage, people are surprised to learn that it is a drug, a powerful drug that can cause dependence and illness. The truth is that coffee is a strong stimulant. Some people suffer withdrawal symptoms if they stop drinking coffee suddenly.

Other caffeine beverages don't seem to be as powerful or as harmful as coffee. Tea is not as irritating to the body, and cases of dependence on tea are less common. This is probably because there are other elements in coffee that increase the stimulating effect.

Tea, however, *is* a stimulant, and enough of it will make you jittery and unable to get to sleep.

Cola (or kola) is a caffeine-containing seed or nut from the kola tree. In African countries where the trees grow, people chew the nuts for their stimulating effect. Bottled "cola" drinks have very little kola nut included and, though these drinks do contain caffeine, it is either synthetic caffeine or caffeine extracted from coffee.

The national drink of Brazil is guarana, made from the seeds of a jungle shrub. It contains more caffeine than coffee.

In Argentina, the most popular caffeine drink is mate, which is made from the leaves of the holly plant. It is used in some breakfast teas available in the states. Celestial Seasonings' *Morning Thunder* is one.

One reason for the popularity of caffeine-containing beverages is that they give you temporary control over energy and the ups and downs of moods. If you are willing to pay the price, and then let the body recharge itself, there is nothing wrong with drinking a stimulating beverage now and then.

You can use L-phenylalanine, L-tyrosine, or other amino acids and get the same rewards with much less damage to your system. (Refer back to chapter two.) The production of neurotransmitters can be better controlled with amino acids than with caffeine.

Yohimbe or Yohimbine

This substance has been touted as an aphrodisiac and an effective remedy for human impotence for centuries. Its reputation was considered to be a folk tale until it began to be studied scientifically, and then the herb hit the fan.

Stanford University called it a "true aphrodisiac."

Science Digest heralded it as "a cure for impotence."

Time magazine described it as "touted for years as an aphrodisiac."

Stanford scientists wrote that yohimbe may be a true aphrodisiac, since, in experiments with rats, it increases arousal in sexually experienced male rats, facilitates copulatory behavior in sexually naive males, and induces sexual activity in male rats that were previously sexually inactive.

According to other research done by Doctors Alvaro Morales and David Surrige of Queen's University in Ontario, yohimbe causes sexual arousal and erection by increasing the flow of blood directly to the penis. It also influences the flexibility of the muscles so they can become firm and rigid. This means very little sexual stimulation is necessary to produce a full erection.

This stimulant is derived primarily from the bark of a West African tree called *Pausinystalia* or *Corynanthe yohimbe*, though it is also present in other species of *Corynanthe* and in *Aspidosperma quebranchoblanco* and *Mitragnya stipulosa*.

Yohimbe is actually a drug. When this alkaloid is brewed as a tea, its effects usually come on in forty-five minutes to an hour. There is an increase in vasodilation and peripheral blood flow, along with stimulation of the spinal ganglia that control erectile tissue, followed by slight "hallucinogenic effects" that last for about two hours. Users may then easily fall asleep.

CAUTION: Anyone with diabetes, kidney or heart disease should not experiment with yohimbe. It should not be used in combination with amphetamines or other stimulants. Avoid chocolate, cheese, sherry, bananas, pineapples, sauerkraut, and other foods containing tyramine for twelve hours before and after using. The combination can cause a dangerous rise in blood pressure.

To make a yohimbe sex-stimulating cocktail, get some powdered bark at your herb shop.

Simmer three to five teaspoons of powdered herb in a pint of water. Use a low dose for the first time.

As the solution cools, add one thousand milligrams of vitamin C to the mixture.

Add honey for flavor, and sip.

Vitamin C is added to make a compound called yohimbine

ascorbate. It is a milder form of yohimbe and more of a nutritional product.

When yohimbe is combined with hydrochloric acid, a different, more dangerous compound is formed that is much more of a hallucinogenic agent and acts more strongly on the brain. *It is not recommended for use by humans.*

You may want to check with your doctor first before you begin experimenting with this African alkaloid. He can look up any side effects that may conflict with existing conditions.

Kava-Kava

Kava-Kava comes from the root pulp and lower stems of a tall perennial shrub found in the South Pacific Islands. The plant, *Piper methsyticum*, grows best near sea level in areas like the Solomon Islands, Fiji, Samoa, Tahiti, and New Guinea.

The stimulating ingredients are in the roots. With sufficient sunlight and three to four years' growth, the roots can be three to five inches thick. Older plants have roots that are heavy, knotted, and strong. After twenty years of growing, they may weigh as much as one hundred pounds. When harvested, the roots are scraped and cut into pieces that are then either chewed (the Tonga method) or crushed between rocks (the Fiji method).

We are more civilized and can use a blender. Here's one recipe for a Kava-Kava cocktail:

Put one ounce of the chopped or ground root into a blender. Add:

2 tablespoons vegetable oil
1 tablespoon lecithin granules or flakes
½ cup skim milk
½ cup water
Some chopped ice

Blend thoroughly and strain before drinking. This should make two cups of brew.

The cocktail produces a climate of warmth and is stimulating to the genital area. Be ready to begin your amorous Kava-Kava adventure, because in an hour you will be happily asleep.

It is said that the oil of the Kava-kava helps control premature ejaculation. The oil, patted on the head of the penis, permits greater control and a much more leisurely buildup. It should enable easier penetration and longer control over orgasm.

Kava-Kava's action is attributed to a collection of alpha pyrones: kawain, dihydrokawain, methysticin, dihydromethysticin, yangonin, and dihydroyangonin. None of them is soluble in water, but the blender beats them into an emulsion. The milky appearance tells you when the mixture is ready to drink.

Of course if you would rather chew it the way they do in the islands, forget the blender!

Damiana

This herb was known and used by the ancient Aztecs as a tonic, an aphrodisiac, and a cure for impotence. It is known as *Turnera diffeusa* or *Turnera aphrodisiaca* to botanists, and contains damianin, which directly stimulates nerves and sexual organs. The compound is related to the poison strychnine, but offers comparative safety from strychnine's danger.

Livestock breeders have used it to stimulate their studs. A Philadelphia physician, W. H. Meyers, M. D., after giving his impotent patients fifteen drops of damiana extract a day, reported it to be most effective, and the only remedy that had given successful results in all cases.

Damiana tea can be made as follows:

Place two tablespoons of the dried herb in a cup
Add hot water and let steep for five minutes
Strain
Slowly sip the brew.

No more than one cup of tea a day is recommended, since too much can have a bad effect on the liver.

Health food stores sell many of the herbs and stimulants we have discussed and will discuss in this chapter: yohimbe, damiana, kava-kava, guarana, ginseng, gotu-kola, licorice, and sarsaparilla. As more advice to the over-forty male about his sexual pursuits begins to filter into the press, other herbs will surface from their jungle habitats and be offered for sale. If you are ever tempted to try them, begin with half or less than the recommended dose and be very cautious.

Here are some of the more obscure "aphrodisiacs" being used in the "uncivilized" parts of the world, as revealed by ethnopharmacologists:

Ric, leaf juice used in the Caroline Islands to promote erection.

Jatropha angusta, a Peruvian plant to stimulate desire.

Anadenanthera colubrina, seeds boiled in water with honey to inflame the desires of older males.

Momordica charantia, a Mexican wild cucumber nicknamed the "Love Spreader."

Babchi, from India, contains the alkaloid psoralein and is used for impotence.

Epimedium macranthum, from the Chinese interior, restores potency and fertility.

Gotu-kola

Centella asiatica, two leaves a day keeps old age away, says the legend, and millions of Chinese agree.

A daily cup of tea made with a teaspoon or two of the herb is an excellent tonic for the nerves, the brain, and the hormonal system. It helps digestion, and may improve resistance to disease and aging. If sexual energy is on the wane, it is said to be able to boost vitality.

Licorice

This is one of the most frequently prescribed herbs in Chinese medicine, although it is no stranger to the Western world. We know it mainly as the flavor in "licorice" candy (which is really the flavor of anise — star anise — and not licorice at all). Licorice is *Glycyrrhiza glabra* or one of the other varieties of the plant. It contains over one hundred fifty medicinal compounds. Its medicinal effects include the ability to reduce blood cholesterol, fever, and inflammation; to promote wound-healing; to increase bile secretion; to be an antitussive, antiulcer, antibacterial, antiallergenic, and to inhibit the growth of experimentally induced tumors.

Licorice contains, as one of its ingredients, estrogenic substances which account for its use as a sexual stimulant. A combination of licorice, milk, and honey has been prescribed as being an aid to a fatigued gentleman.

Sarsaparilla

Smilax officinalis is the dried root of a genus of climbing or trailing vines or shrubs native to tropical America.

The *New York Times*, August 11, 1946, carried the story of a discovery in Mexico of a male hormone in sarsaparilla. Testosterone is present in this plant. Also, progesterone and cirtin are two other hormones that have been isolated from sarsaparilla.

The inability of a man to exercise his normal sex functions may alter his personality and distort his entire outlook on life. He can develop an inferiority complex as he begins to think of himself as less than a man. If the impotence is the result of the inability of the testicles to supply the body with a normal supply of male hormone, administration of testosterone may restore sexual power, mental alertness, and physical strength to men who are entering the aging process of physical decline.

According to Adam Gottlieb in *Sex Drugs and Aphrodisiacs* (San Francisco: The 20th Century Alchemist/High Times/Level

Press, 1974), the following is a sure, though perhaps temporary cure, for a lax libido caused by an insufficiency of hormones:

Take up to one half ounce of the shaved inner sarsaparilla bark,
Put into a large pan with one pint of water,
Let simmer for five to ten minutes.
Be careful to see that it doesn't boil over, because the saponins in the bark can create a large head of foam.
Strain.
Drink a cup morning and night, swirling the liquid around in your mouth before you swallow it.
Or, you can make a tincture by taking a bottle and filling it with one-half sarsaparilla, one-fourth water, and one-fourth vodka.
Let it stand for two weeks, making sure to shake it once or twice a day.
At the end of the time, you have a drink to support your lazy glands. Take a tablespoonful three times a day.

Don't rely on this remedy for more than a few weeks at a time. There is some evidence that the external use of such hormones may lead the body to shut down its own production of chemicals. You want to spark your own organs into renewed life and not become dependent on a substitute!

Ginseng

This rare and expensive medicinal root has shown promise in combatting senility.

Pharmacologist Dr. Jelleff Carr of the University of Maryland states that the discovery of the chemical constituents of ginseng, ginsenosides, holds exciting possibilities. Its properties seem to enhance mental and physical abilities.

A German study group looked at the effects of ginseng on the elderly. An extract was administered orally for three months. They reported a decrease in the rigidity of aging, an increase in alertness and the powers of concentration, improved visual-motor co-ordination, improved grasp of abstract concepts, and similar behavioral changes, Carr said.

In addition, a Soviet study of young athletes showed increased performance capability and greater ease in performing work. Males forty to sixty years old showed significant respiratory improvement after twelve weeks of treatment.

The clinical reports suggest beneficial effects from ginseng upon physical and intellectual performance in the young athlete and the older subject suffering from the deficits of aging, according to Carr.

Doctor Carr, who takes ginseng, said it must be taken for about a month before benefits can be felt.

"It can conceivably be a tremendous thing in the coming years."

Ginseng, also known as "Miracle Root," and "Root of Life," is a native of China and North America. It has been extolled as everything from an aphrodisiac to a digestive aid. The Chinese believe it can prolong life, and our Native Americans once thought it had magical powers.

Jen-Shen, the Chinese word for ginseng, means "sacred man-root." Its healing qualities have been known in China for over five thousand years, and it is now being investigated in the United States.

Many of our common health foods came originally from Asia:

The apricot originated in China, was cultivated in Spain, and was brought to the west coast of the United States with the Spanish explorers.

Soybean is another gift from China to the Western world. It is a rich source of protein, high in calcium and phosphorus.

Sesame seeds, initially used in China as a snack or as a paste, is extremely high in calcium and provides impressive amounts of iron, protein, and phosphorus.

The Chinese bitter melon stimulates the appetite and aids in digestion. It is also a good source of vitamin A, B1 and B2.

The lotus root, used as a food and a tonic, is rich in vitamin C. The seeds are used to preserve strength, promote circulation, and to strengthen virility.

Dragon's Eye (loong ngan) is related to the lichee.
It is very high in iron content and is considered to be an antifatigue
agent.

A Barefoot Doctor's Manual, the paramedic book of China,
devotes 372 pages to discussing 522 *common* Chinese herbs of the over
eight thousand in usage. The most famous of them is ginseng.

Richard P. Huemer, M.D., conducted research on the Asiatic
variety (*Panax ginseng*) with his associate Kyung-Dong Lee. The
work was done on mice and transplantable tumors. In five out of
seven trials there was significant slowing in tumor growth. Ginseng
also enhanced the ability of laboratory animals to withstand stress,
promoted recovery in cases of hemorrhage, and lowered blood sugar
in diabetic mice.

Recent investigations also reveal that in the body, ginseng appears
to do the work of certain hormones secreted by the adrenal cortex. As
a result, the brain does not have to work as hard, and does not need to
manufacture large amounts of these substances.

According to Richard Heffern in *The Complete Book of Ginseng*,
animal studies have illustrated that laboratory rats fed ginseng live an
average of 109 days longer than rats given none. This amounts to
about ten years in human terms.

Norman Farnsworth, Ph.D., a professor of pharmacognosy at the
University of Illinois in Chicago, has studied ginseng at length. He
states, "*People are beginning to understand that there are things that
can improve the body without using harsh chemicals. Gingeng is one.
We think ginseng probably induces the body to produce interferon,
then the interferon protects the body.*"

Ginseng contains at least six glycosides (called panaxoxides or
ginsenosides), and at least six sapogenins attached to the glycosides.
In combination, these: increase endocrine activity, increase
metabolic rate, stimulate the circulatory system and the digestive
system, maintain the general equilibrium of the body, and *prevent
adverse reaction to stress*.

Ginseng also contains phosphorus, iron, copper, magnesium,
potassium, sulfur, manganese, and silica. The enzymes amylase and
phenolase are also present, as are vitamins B1 and B2.

Each person seeks to live as long as possible. To reach this goal, intervention measures have been developed, aimed at obtaining the psychological and physical well-being of the aging human.

These are: Prevention of pathological disturbances, age fatigue, and loss of vitality; correction of existing damages; and rehabilitation of the body.

The substance which can accomplish these three goals would have to be an "adaptogen." An adaptogen is able to increase the general capability of the organism to overcome internal and external stress by adaptation. Ginseng is an adaptogen.

According to a study done by U.J. Schmidt et al., *Pharmacotherapy and Basic Therapy in Old Age*, August 20, 1978, which was part of the Gerontological Research Project of the German Democratic Republic, ginseng was given over a period of one hundred days to 540 patients, age sixty and up. The ginseng was "Ginsanna" brand in capsule form. During the first thirty days, two capsules were given daily. After that, one capsule was administered every day.

The results were compared to a control group and the individuals receiving the "Ginsanna" showed the following positive results: improvement of metabolism and liver function; stabilization of blood sugar; stabilization of blood pressure; enhancement of blood circulation in the heart, brain, and other organs; and increase of mental and physical performance.

Professor Petkov of the Institute of Advanced Medical Training in Sofia has demonstrated that ginseng actually increases the brain's efficiency. Ginseng stimulates the basic neural processes which constitute the functioning of the cerebral cortex, namely the excitation and inhibition, which form the physiological basis of man's functioning as a whole.

Ginseng, however, unlike stimulants such as amphetamine, causes no disturbance in the equilibrium of the cerebral process. It doesn't provoke subjective excitement and does not interfere with normal bodily functions such as sleep.

According to the *Barefoot Doctor's Manual*, ginseng should be used for a deficiency of energy and blood; internal injuries caused by worry; convalescent weakness; lack of appetite; palpitations; impotency; insomnia; and forgetfulness.

With a little stretch of the imagination, these conditions could apply to most of the over forty group anywhere in the world.

Evening Primrose

Recharge Your Battery

Tired, run down, feel sexy, but it's too much trouble?

Can you relate to this sentence?

Then this is your chapter.

Are you taking all of your vitamins and minerals, eating a balanced diet, drinking eight glasses of water a day, getting plenty of rest, keeping regular by eating lots of fiber?

But still prefer watching to doing?

Maybe you need vitamin B15!

Vitamin B15 is not really a vitamin. It is a natural substance found in some foods, but it's not a vitamin because it doesn't fit the FDA's definition of what a vitamin should be.

If a vitamin is deficient in the body it causes a definite set of symptoms. For example, vitamin A deficiency causes night blindness.

If vitamin B15 is deficient, there's no way to tell.

So, vitamin B15 is not a vitamin.

It has been around as a separate factor since 1951, when Doctor Ernest T. Krebs Sr. isolated it from apricot pits.

Chemically, it is N'-N dimethylgycine. It's also been called pangamic acid, and has been the subject of a lot of controversy and confusion. The FDA has waged a war against it, possibly because it was found by Dr. Krebs, who also introduced Laetrile to the world.

The obsessive attack against the sale of B15 caused a number of bogus products to be offered to the public, who learned about it and wanted to buy it.

The FDA tried to ban the sale, but the court disagreed. But, the FDA won a partial victory when they had it classified as a food additive, even though it is found in nature and can be manufactured in the body in small quantities.

Since it was classified as a food additive, however, that gives the FDA the right to restrict its use if it is combined with any other substance.

That makes it a strange law!

It is all right to sell if it's sold alone, but if it's mixed with anything — then it's illegal to sell.

But, if you want to get some, the Da Vinci Company packs tiny tablets of B15 in foil. You can buy it from most health food stores. You may have to ask them to order it for you, but it is available.

Why am I bothering with a substance that's so hard to obtain?

Because it does things you may want done to your body.

B15 (DMG — dimethylglycine) was used (in a mixture along with honey and vitamin B12) by Muhammad Ali when he regained his heavyweight title.

You may not want to go into the ring, but you sure want to be a champ again in bed!

Other athletes using DMG have been the Dallas Cowboys, the Pittsburgh Steelers, and the New York Yankees.

They say that DMG improves the use of oxygen in the body, which increases the body's stamina and energy.

If it helps in football and baseball, consider what it can do in the game of love!

If it's not a vitamin, just what is it?

The answer emerging from a study of its chemistry is that it is not a single substance but a mixture of ingredients, gluconic acid and dimethylglycine.

One of its activities is to detoxify free radicals, which attack sensitive genital tissue and other cells.

The Soviet Union has been using DMG combined with calcium gluconate as part of the training program for the Olympic Games. This combination is forbidden by the FDA since any combination of DMG and any other substance, including vitamins, is a violation.

However, there may be a way around this irrational judgment. There is another substance called trimethylglycine (TMG). It is identical to DMG except that its chemistry adds a group, a methyl group, so it's *tri* instead of *di*.

When it is ingested, the body removes a methyl group and coverts the TMG into DMG. It's that simple!

The work is done in the liver and the result is energy and an additional attack on the free radicals.

TMG is also called betaine.

Be careful. Betaine is sold as betaine hydrochloride in health food stores *but that is not the form you want*.

Betaine hydrochloride is sold as an aid to people who have weak digestive juices, not enough hydrochloric acid in their stomachs. It is acidic, must be taken with meals or it can cause gastic irritation. This is not what you are looking for.

You want pure betaine, also known as free-base betaine. It is slightly sweet to the taste and will not hurt you.

For more on this subject, refer to: Paul G. Schultz, "Dimethylglycine and Vitamin B15," *Los Angeles College of Chiropractic News and Alumni Report*, December 1979; B. Grzelakowska-Sztabert and M. Balinska, *Biochim. Biophys. Acta.*, 632:164-72 (1980); A. J. Barak, N. J. Tuna, and S. Berlow, *J. Ped.*, 99:467-72 (1981); D. Wilken, et al., *New England Journal of Medicine*, 309:448-53 (1983).

Is DMG [or TMG] the answer to your energy problem?

Although these substances do not actually stimulate the sexual organs as other substances do, they do appear to increase the oxygen-carrying capacity of the blood. Oxygen delivers energy to muscles. Muscles become fatigued when there is too little oxygen available and too much waste material. If the condition continues, extreme fatigue settles in and you may not even want to move because it's too much effort.

Sexual fatigue may be a result of a lack of energy-boosting oxygen.

Try one tablet to see how it affects your fatigue-factor.

Make a mixture of a tablespoonful of honey, five hundred micrograms of vitamin B12, one tablet of DMG. This is what Muhammad Ali did; then make love, not war!

Energy is not the only product of this non-vitamin. It also helps you to build immunity and resist degenerative disease. If feeling good and healthy is not a big boost to sex then nothing is!

According to a report in the *Journal of Infectious Diseases*, January 1981, written by Doctor Charles D. Graber of the University of South Carolina School of Medicine, the use of DMG enhanced both antibody production and cellular immunity in humans. In a double-blind test study, where two groups were used and neither group knew which one had gotten the DMG, the test group with the DMG showed improved immunity against disease.

The dose used was less than one hundred milligrams a day.

The immune system protects us against bacteria, viruses, cancer-causing agents, and so on.

The immune system is a complex network of white blood cells (lymphocytes), large scavenger white blood cells (macrophages), antibodies (proteins that can react with specific germs), and interferon (antiviral and antitumor compound). The immune system produces three types of lymphocytes called T-cells, B-cells, and K-cells.

Dr. Graber's research has shown that DMG significantly stimulates B-cells to produce a much higher antibody response and enhances the activity of T-cells and macrophages.

Strengthening the immune system means increasing resistance to disease caused by viruses, bacteria, fungi, and even cancer.

In addition to boosting our immune response, and the amount of energy we can get from available oxygen in the blood stream, Dr. Jerzy W. Meduski of the Nutritional Research Laboratories, USC School of Medicine in Los Angeles, says DMG will help people with diminished blood flow due to arteriosclerosis or other circulatory problems.

It's not only for humans either!

James Gannon, DVM, of the University of Melbourne, Australia, found DMG to be effective in improving the racing time of trained greyhounds.

So there you have the story. I don't know why the FDA is against the use of DMG. If there is a real danger, it should be removed from the shelves and banned from manufacture or sale. To simply call it a food additive, and permit its sale in one form but not in another, appears to be nothing more than politics. Politics should have no place in preventive medicine or any other form of medicine.

You want to get more oxygen into your life, and DMG may be one of the ways to do it, but you can't depend on DMG to do the job by itself. You could live, give or take, about two months without food and perhaps a few days without water but only about five minutes without the breath of life—oxygen!

Every cell, every tissue needs to be bathed in oxygen constantly, so why eat foods that interfere with the flow of blood that carries the oxygen around the body?

Don Mannerberg, M. D., in a book he coauthored called *Aerobic Nutrition*, maintains that the standard American diet impedes the transport of oxygen to the cells by overloading the blood with fat. Just breathing will get air into the lungs, but that only begins the process. Now the oxygen has to be picked up and transported to areas all over the body, including the brain, where thoughts of sex begin, and to the sex organs, where the thoughts are carried out.

If your diet is too high in fat, concentrated sugars, and too much alcohol, tryglycerides reach high blood levels and can cause havoc in the red blood cell transport system. This affects the non-muscular parts of the body first. That includes the brain, liver, and kidneys. They can't exercise to get more oxygen, so partial oxygen starvation eventually produces degenerative diseases.

Currently, the average American diet derives about forty-two percent of its calories from fat and about another seventeen percent from refined sugars. Add about another seven percent from alcohol, and you find that two-thirds of the calories are in forms that are virtually devoid of the nutrients the body really needs.

Add smoke from a pack of cigarettes, yours or someone else's smoke, and there are other troubles. Because of tar, smoking reduces oxygen levels in the blood by decreasing the amount of oxygen the lungs can absorb. Smoking also decreases the amount of oxygen the blood can carry by tying up the red blood cells with carbon monoxide. And, for a kicker, there's the fact that nicotine constricts capillaries, making it more difficult for the blood to reach the tissues.

Therefore, unless you're willing to help yourself by paying a bit more attention to your oxygen supply, why are you reading this book?

Dr. Carlton Fredericks, probably the dean of nutritional research, has dealt at great length with products such as wheat germ and vitamin E, and their links to sex power. In his book *Food Facts and Fallacies*, he explains that, although vitamin E has been linked to sex, it is really other factors in wheat germ oil that are responsible for energy and increased sexual capacity. The factor referred to is called octaconsanol.

Octaconsanol really appears to be an aphrodisiac. It steps up the production of semen in men and it provides extra energy to further aid the performance.

Although you may not want to have any more babies and do not think that an increased production of semen is helpful to your sexual function, when the testicles are full, the desire to empty them is increased. The body and the mind do not know you don't want to make a baby. They're interested in keeping the race going and will reward you with a very pleasing orgasm each time you engage in sex.

Researchers argue that the mere production of more testosterone (the male hormone) in the male body does not of itself increase sex, that sex is in great measure a mental attitude. The latter is true, but the support suggested in this book is both hormonal and multifactorial. Therefore, any nutritional or supplemental approach that stimulates the increased production of sperm, increased energy, and increased oxygen supplies should logically step up a male's interest in getting rid of the excess sperm!

Octacosanol is, in itself, multifactorial. It can relax muscles, provide a feeling of well-being, step up reaction time, actuity, and other biological functions—including production of sperm. In other words, it provides more of the total mechanism involved in the sex act.

There is speculation that octacosanol stimulates the pituitary gland, the master gland of the body, which controls almost everything. If we want to live longer, better, sexier lives we have to step up the effectiveness of this little factory at the base of the brain.

Animal evidence is available concerning the ability of octacosanol to stimulate sexuality. Marinetti found that it is closely related to an animal enzyme with a high male hormone action. Levin and Dorfman found octacosanol highly significant as a male hormone in chickens; Dukelow in sows; Farrell in rats; Vogt-Moeller in cattle and humans. Sorry to link us with cattle, but sex is sex!

Octacosanol is an energy booster, but it contrasts strongly with the type of energy obtained from other substances, like caffeine. Caffeine can increase energy, but it increases muscle tension and elevates blood pressure at the same time.

Octacosanol relaxes the muscles, steps up reflex action and acuity, and lowers blood pressure as it does so. The relaxing effect on the muscles means relief from nervous tension. When muscles tighten, as in stress, they get ready for physical action—flight or fight—and the blood vessels constrict and blood pressure rises. If you have to choose between caffeine and octacosanol, make the right choice.

What is this substance we're talking about?

Is it some new drug from a laboratory that has labored for five years, that has cost millions in research, that has been approved by the FDA, and that you have to get a prescription for?

No! It's a natural substance found in the germ of wheat. Wheat germ is the embryo of the wheat kernel, which contains vitamins, minerals, sex hormones, vitamin E, and various essential poly-unsaturated fats.

It is the oil in the wheat germ that contains the octacosanol, but in tiny quantities, and, although you should have wheat germ in the form of whole wheat bread daily, the best way to get octacosanol is from supplements.

There is an entire book, a 532 page report, by Doctor Thomas Kirk Cureton, the primary researcher into the magic of octacosanol. *The Physiological Effects of Wheat Germ Oil in Human Exercise* is avilable for those who want to explore the initial efforts to under-stand nutrition and energy-gain from wheat germ and its com-ponents.

Octacosanol enables the body to maintain high activity for a longer span of time. If you take it too close to bedtime, it may keep you awake a bit longer than average. If you tend to nod off after dinner this may be a boon to you and your wife. It is an individual reaction, and you'll discover soon enough how to use it and when to use it. It can be used every day without any harm to the user.

Some people report that combinations of octacosanol with other natural supplements such as dessicated liver, vitamin B6, selenium, and chromium do keep them up later than they wish, so take these combined forms during the day—for a matinee!

In *Psycho-dietetics* the distinguished researchers, Doctors E. Cheraskin and W. M. Ringsdorf, Jr., observe that individuals with hypoglycemia (low blood sugar), who are troubled by excess fatigue, may benefit from a wheat germ oil supplement and, further, they comment that if a person has been eating regularly and properly and exercising regularly and properly, yet still has trouble reaching a high degree of physical fitness, the missing element might be octacosanol.

They add that octacosanol improves stamina, endurance, reduces heart stress, and quickens reaction time.

I couldn't say it better myself.

Octacosanol is available at all health food stores and drugstores.

Adenosine triphosphate (ATP) is the substance which stores energy that is created when the body burns carbohydrates and fats. When energy is needed by the body, as in muscular contraction, ATP is broken down to release the stored energy.

Although we have the capacity to manufacture certain nutrients, it is sometimes more cost-effective to take them in supplement form. Rats, for example, have the ability to manufacture their own vitamin C, which we can't do. However, if the rat is given supplementary vitamin C as well as the amount he can manufacture, he can withstand a greater amount of stress than if he had to depend only on his own manufacturing ability.

General stamina can be greatly increased in a short amount of time. Calcium pantothenate is an anti-stress vitamin. It can increase total muscular output (stamina). Rats given calcium pantothenate or pantothenic acid greatly increase their total muscular work output. It plays the same role in humans as it does in the laboratory animal. It is needed to metabolize fats and carbohydrates into energy, water, and carbon dioxide.

It is possible that low energy is a result of a deficiency of pantothenic acid. *It may also be a result of diabetes, anemia, or some other condition, so check with your doctor.*

The amino acid L-phenylalanine is also useful in restoring energy and vitality, especially after stressful activity. Stress and overwork can deplete noradrenaline, resulting in mental fatigue and loss of concentration. The use of the amino acid L-phenylalanine helps your brain replace the lost neurotransmitter. If you feel mentally drained, you may have used up more of the noradrenaline than your diet has supplied the raw materials for. In that case your brain needs additional material to begin to manufacture norepinephrine again. You can refill your battery by using this amino acid. Make sure you have enough vitamin B6 and vitamin C available for the conversion of L-phenylalanine to noradrenaline. The amino acid L-tyrosine can act in the same manner. You don't *have* to drag yourself out of bed in the morning.

Take a tip from professional athletes who use nutrients to get their body in shape for sporting events. You can do the same for life-events.

Dr. Bernard Friedlander, a specialist in sports medicine in Santa Monica, California, is convinced that nutrition is the way to go. He advises fresh fruit, poultry or fish, eggs, whole grain cereals, spring water, and herb teas. His nutritional program also includes vitamin and mineral supplementaion, bee pollen, octacosanol, glandulars, and amino acids.

Antioxidants are also important for your performance, since they prevent cellular damage by destroying harmful free radicals. You can protect your body with vitamins A (Beta-caroten), B1, B5, B6, para amino benzoic acid (PABA), C, E, selenium, and zinc, amino acids cysteine and methionine, L-glutathione, Superoxide dismutase (SOD), catalase, the bioflavonoids, and gamma oryzanol.

The amino acid L-carnitine is necessary for transporting fatty acids into the mitochondria (energy-producing apparatus in each cell). When there is a deficiency of this substance, which can be manufactured in the body, providing all of the raw materials in the diet, supplementation can be of great value.

Coenzyme Q-10 is another nutrient necessary for energy. It is needed for ATP formation and is used as a cardiovascular aid in Japan.

The gamma oryzanol mentioned above is derived from rice bran oil. It is an antioxidant and helps to improve liver function and lower cholesterol. It is found in health food stores in certain formulas, but not usually found alone. You can locate it if you read enough labels.

Cytochrome-C is a combination of amino acids and iron that helps muscles to recover from fatigue. Like gamma oryzanol, it is seldom found alone, but only as part of an antifatigue formula.

Propolis, another element from the life of the bee, has become a valuable tool for healthful living. It is a remarkable natural antibiotic that helps to fight disease reactions in the body. It even helps control runaway cell breakdown.

Bee propolis is a resinous material gathered by bees from the leaf buds and bark of trees. The poplar tree is most sought after by the bees. The bees seal holes and cracks in the hive with this sticky substance. They also use it to coat the cells in which the queen bee will lay her eggs. This coating will make the cell a sterile environment. A bee hive is a very busy place with nearly 100,000 bees living, working, and caring for young bees. It should be full of bacteria, but is a nearly sterile environment because of the activity of bee propolis.

Unlike penicillan and other drugs, propolis does not appear to damage helpful organisms, and viruses do not build up an immunity to it.

As a natural therapeutic, the action of propolis may well be attributed to its concentration of bioflavonoids, a group of plant compounds that work closely with vitamin C. Currently, bioflavonoids are recognized as being able to heal the capillary system, to help mend the fragility of the tiny blood vessels, and to act as a vasodilator and diuretic.

Propolis is also a source of histamine, a substance greatly involved in orgasm.

According to Roy Kupsinel, M.D., Maitland, Florida, propolis is a healer. He prescribes it as a safe nutritional supplement to create a disease-fighting reaction against almost any illness, without dangerous side effects.

John Diamond, M.D., of Valley Cottage, N.Y., one time president of the International Academy of Preventive Medicine, says the substance activates the thymus gland and, therefore, the immune system.

L-glutamine is the amide form of glutamic acid. This doesn't mean much to you until an explanation is made about the brain and its source of energy. The brain governs how you feel about many things, including sex. A well-fed brain will manufacture transmitters for healthy conduct of all body activity. But, what does the brain eat?

The brain eats only two substances, glucose and glutamic acid! Glucose finds its way past the brain-barrier with ease, but, glutamic acid can't. Due to some mix-up a few hundred thousand years ago, the brain-barrier will not let it through. However, it will let its cousin, L-glutamine, into the brain area without any objections. Once L-glutamine is in the brain area, the brain converts it to glutamic acid and has a feast.

What this offers the nutritional scientist is another way to manipulate brain energy. For example, people with a craving for alcohol (or candy, for that matter) appear to be in need of brain fuel. Alcohol is easily converted to glucose, and candy is loaded with it. If the brain is given L-glutamine instead, the craving soon subsides.

Will L-glutamine provide you with more energy for sexual pursuits? If your brain is hungry for energy, this amino acid will provide it!

Carnitine was mentioned previously. It is important to say that the L-carnitine form is the only form to be taken as a supplement. Neither the D-carnitine nor a combination of L- and D-carnitine should be used in supplement form.

Carnitine is an unusual amino acid that is manufactured in the liver of humans and is present in muscle and organ meats in usual diets. Carnitine is not found in vegetables or grains. In human metabolism it transfers fatty acids across the membranes of the mitochrondria to be used as a source of fuel.

If there is a deficiency of this amino acid, fatty acids are poorly metabolized and can build up inside the cell or in the surrounding area, leading to elevated levels of blood fat and tryglyceride.

Carnitine is not a vitamin, because it can be manufactured in the body. It is not an essential amino acid for the same reason. It can be made from two other amino acids, lysine and methionine, as long as there are enough vitamins C, B6 and B3 present.

Men have higher levels of carnitine than women do. High levels of carnitine are found in the epididymis of the testes of men. Adequate levels of carnitine are necessary for energy metabolism within the sperm to ensure proper motility.

Your blender can help you to prepare many invigorating drinks from foods or from combinations of foods and supplements.

For example:

Try the following drink for a lift in midafternoon. Use your juicer to make the juice first, then blend well. It takes a little time to make, but the effects are worth it and will lead you to try other natural combinations when you feel the difference!

2 tablespoons apple cider vinegar
¼ cup cucumber juice
¼ cup lettuce juice
½ cup carrot juice
4 tablespoons cold pressed wheat germ oil

The combination of nutrients in this fresh vegetable juice, plus the nutrients in wheat germ oil, can make you feel better than you have in years.

Or try this mixture before meals:

2 tablespoons apple cider vinegar
2 tablespoons cold pressed seed oil (any variety)
¼ cup apple juice
¼ cup grapefruit juice
¼ cup orange juice

Drink this mixture one hour before meals to perk up your digestive system.

Phosphorus occurs in natural form in many vegetables. This mixture, while somewhat strong-tasting, is a prime source of minerals to aid in muscle contraction, glandular secretion, and nerve impulse transformation.

Mix well:

3 ounces carrot juice
2 ounces celery juice
1 ounce radish juice
1 tablespoon onion juice

If you're still working, try this instead of a coffee break. You'll be amazed at the energy this drink gives compared to your usual coffee.

If fatigue is one of your problems, and you suspect that you may not have enough iron in your diet, put this mixture together and drink a few cups daily until you feel as strong as iron again:

½ cup raisin juice
½ cup apricot juice
1 teaspoon lemon juice

Juices are best when they are fresh. Sip them immediately after making. Once you store them, even in a cool place, they begin to lose food values almost at once. It pays to buy a good juicer and a good blender.

Another pick-me-up is a blend of ½ cabbage juice and ½ tomato juice. Add a dash of kelp powder to spark the flavor. This mixture provides minerals that follow a path straight to the thyroid gland. Once there, the gland prepares thyroxin, and youthful energy is the result.

Potassium is one of the nutrient minerals for the look and feel of youth. Diuretics (drugs or foods that promote a flow of urine) can deplete the body of some of its potassium stores and make a person feel old and unresponsive.

Try this unusual combination to help your potassium level remain normal:

Get a batch of sun-dried fruits like apricots, prunes, pears, raisins, and peaches. Make sure they have not been treated with sulfur dioxide.

Put them in a glass bowl.

Heat a pot of water to boiling, then let the boiling quiet down.

Pour enough boiled water into the bowl to cover the fruit.

Cover the bowl and let stand at room temperature overnight.

The next morning, pour off a cup and drink it before breakfast. You can store the rest of the juice in the fridge and eat the fruit.

You will get the benefits of all the minerals, plus the added benefit of the laxative quality of the mixture.

Desiccated liver was mentioned in this book as one of the better energy-packed foods. It does have a liver taste that turns many people away from it. But, it is so useful that the following mixture will allow even the most confirmed liver-hater to use it profitably:

¼ teaspoon desiccated liver powder
Glass of tomato juice (without salt)
1 teaspoon lemon juice
Blend well and drink twice a day.

Although part of the power of this drink comes from vitamins and minerals, more comes from the amino acid content. Liver, being a complete protein, offers quantities of all of the essential amino acids. Because it is defatted and dried, desiccated liver powder helps to feed the body and the brain.

Carlson Wade in his book, *Health Tonics, Elixirs and Potions for the Look and Feel of Youth*, Arco Publishing Co., N.Y., tells about three herbal-spice aphrodisiac mixtures.

Don Juan's Special Love Potion

1 cup tomato juice
¼ teaspoon basil leaves, finely crushed
Drink one hour before seduction

Casanova Cocktail

¼ teaspoon cinnamon powder
½ cup slightly steamed apple juice
½ cup grapefruit juice
Take three times a day.

Cleopatra Elixir

½ teaspoon ground cloves
½ cup papaya juice
¼ cup watermelon juice
¼ cup banana puree
Blend well and sip slowly.

Who's to say that they don't work? Try them all for yourself. I think the last one is the most effective!

Try this for breakfast and start the day with a matinee!

In your blender or food processer mix:

4 dried apricots
1 teaspoon powdered whey
1 teaspoon blackstrap molasses
1 banana
1 tablespoon soya powder
1 tablespoon brewer's yeast
3 tablespoons raw wheat germ
1 tablespoon granulated or powdered lecithin
Honey to taste

Blend well for about three to five minutes; then sip and enjoy. You'll have pep, vigor, and vitality for any job or pleasure you choose.

Milk is an energy food. When prepared this way, it is even more energizing:

In your blender mix:

1-½ cups milk
1 raw egg yolk
1 pinch kelp
1 teaspoon lemon juice
½ cup fresh apricot juice
Blend for about a minute. Then sip slowly.

From Legend to Prescription

Few men will not be interested in the relationship between food and love through the ages. Doctor Van de Velde, in his book *Ideal Marriage*, realized the value of certain foods for increasing potency in normal males, as well as the utility of these foods in cases of male sexual disorder.

The sexual impulse in the normal healthy male is a strong one. His desire for complete sexual satisfaction is also strong. According to Wilhelm Stekel, a man's self-confidence, for the most part, teeters on his preservation or recovery of sexual potency.

Among the earliest references to aphrodisiacs is the mention of the mandrake (Genesis, Chap. XXX). The Hebrew word *Dudaim* has been translated as "mandrake." *Dudaim* indicates a fruit with a sweet and agreeable odor, much in demand by the male sex. The word is probably derived from *Dudim* which means "pleasures of love." It has also been translated as "apple." Could this have been the apple in the Garden of Eden?

Mandrake or *mandragora officinarum* is a plant of the same family as the potato. Its aphrodisiacal ability is suspect, but it was used as an anaesthetic in earlier times and has been said to be the drink held to the lips of men being cruicified to ease their pain. Too much of the drink caused a stupor and death.

The Perfumed Garden For The Soul's Delectation, translated from the Arabic of the Shaykh Nafzawi by Sir R. F. Burton, is rich in recipes and other details.

The Shaykh's list of eight things that give sexual strength included: Bodily health; the absence of all care and worry; an unembarrassed mind; natural gaiety of the spirit; wealth; the variety of the faces of women; the variety of their complexions; and good nourishment!

The list is as good today as it was in the seventeenth century when the book was written.

The first recipe in *The Garden* reads as follow:

For coital strength, take the fruit of the mastic tree, pound them well and macerate them with oil and honey. Then drink of the liquid first thing in the morning.

A nighttime recipe suggests twenty almonds, a glass of thick honey and a bit of pine.

Still another suggests green peas boiled with onions and then powdered with cinnamon, ginger, and cardamom seed.

Old men should eat stimulant pastry containing honey, ginger, vinegar, garlic, cinnamon, nutmeg, cardamom, long peppers, and Chinese cinnamon.

For precipitate ejaculation the Shayk recommends nutmeg and oliban mixed with honey.

The final chapter regards "strengthening dishes."

"He who makes it a practice to eat every day fasting yolk of eggs without the white part, will find in this aliment an energetic stimulant for coitus. The same is the case with the man who during three days eats of the same with onions."

"He who boils asparagus, and then fries them in fat, and then pours upon them the yolk of eggs with pounded condiments, and eats everyday of this dish will grow very strong for coitus and find in it a stimulus for his amorous desires."

"He who peels onions, puts them into a saucepan with condiments and aromatic substances and fries the mixture with oil and yolks of eggs will acquire a surpassing and invaluable vigour... if he will partake of this dish for several days."

This is profitable for an old man to read as well as for the man in the best of his years.

"Camel's milk mixed with honey causes the virile member to be on alert night and day."

Amazing to find this kind of nutritional advice at so early a date when we, in this century, are just beginning to realize the profound effects diet has on everything we do!

It was not so in 1931 when William J. Robinson, M.D. wrote the book *Treatment of Sexual Impotence in Men and Women*. He was convinced that the diet should be generous and liberal!

"The patient should eat plenty of eggs, oysters, raw and fried, meat and fish. I often make my patients eat two to six raw eggs a day, two or three the first thing in the morning before breakfast, the rest during the day."

He considered saffron, pepper, mustard, cardamom, cinnamon, nutmeg, and ginger as having an "undoubted effect in stimulating the libido, and the erection center."

Doctor Robinson knew that diet could have a profound effect on sex, and that was fifty-six years ago!

In company with many of his predecessors, from Vatsyayana and Nefzawi onwards, he has considerable faith in the erotic virtues of garlic:

"There is one spice or condiment of which I hesitate to speak because it is held in such contempt and disdain in this country. I refer to garlic. There can, however, be no question as to its pronounced *aphrodisiac effect*. In fact, it stands at the head of the list. But many of our Anglo-Saxons would prefer their impotence to the alternative of not having to eat garlic. The nations, however, who have no loathing for the bulb of *Allium sativum*, the Italians and the Jews, for instance, often make use of garlic as an aphrodisiac; some do it without deliberation, instinctively, so to say."

He also found that while onions have a similar effect on sexuality, the result is not as powerful and not as sustained.

E. Podolsky, M.D., author of an article in *Sex Psychology*, a popular sexology periodical, expressed himself this way regarding food:

It is not necessary to resort to potent drugs to arouse the sexual emotion. It is quite possible in a great many cases to do so by natural means. Food has been found of value in this respect. It is now known that there are certain varieties of foods which have a definite effect on sexual desire.

He points out the importance of fish, valued for aphrodisiac reasons by the Egyptians, and used with the same end in mind by the modern French. Truffles come next on his list. He also draws attention to observations made of young people in an educational establishment. It was noticed that they evinced a connection between the intake of fish and cod liver oil and sexual desire. Lecithin was also found to have a similar effect.

With reference to cocoa, Havelock Ellis indicated that it was considered to come within the range of aphrodisiac beverages.

Foods rich in phosphorus, which is associated with nerve metabolism, and those rich in iron are said to stimulate the sexual function. So, too, do curries, chutneys, and hot sauces, by their irritant action.

Doctor Arnold Lorand in *Health and Longevity through Rational Diet*, tells us that since the most remote periods of the existence of man, the eating of fish has been accredited with the act of increasing sexual activity. It was for this reason that the ancient Egyptians forbade the eating of fish by priests.

Other articles of food, particularly eggs and caviar, are also supposed to exert a stimulating action upon sexual activity. It seems quite certain that a plentiful diet, rich in protein, would have an exciting influence upon the sexual function.

Doctor Lorand points out that the rich phosphorus content of fish may be its chief activating princple. According to his own observations, a diet plentiful in eggs and fish greatly improves sexual function.

He mentions truffles, which are also a good source of iron and phosphorus, and includes lobster and crab in his discussion of stimulating foods.

A List Of Food With Generally Recognized Strengthening or Aphrodisiac Properties

Asparagus

Horseradish

Marjoram

Peas

Radishes

Ginger

Lentils

Beetroot

Cinnamon

Beans (kidney)

Tarragon

Nutmeg

Beans (green)

Coriander

Cardamom

Artichokes

Mint

Red pepper

Spinach

Gentian

White pepper

Onions

Saffron

Cubeb

Garlic

Sage

Kola nut

Thyme

Cloves

Paprika

Crab

Animal testes

Lobster

Kidneys

Crayfish

Tripe

Shrimp

Yeast

Oyster

Eggs

Mussels

Banana

Cockles

Peach

Clams

Figs

Herring

Pineapple

Salmon

Cherries

Mackerel

Grapes

Cod Liver

Grape juice

Cod Liver Oil

Tomatoes

Halibut

Roe

Meats

Fowl

Liver

Truffles are first on the list for Brillat-Savarin:

> The tubercle is not only delicious to the taste, but excites a power, the exercise of which is accompanied by the most delicious pleasures... The truffle is a positive aphrodisiac... it makes women more amiable and men more amorous...

In Van de Velde's exhaustive treatise on coital technique and physical adjustment in marriage he included references to an aphrodisiac diet:

> ...Certain books written in the sixteenth and seventeenth centuries describe in minute detail all solid and liquid varieties of nourishment calculated to incite sexual desire (libido), to intensify sexual pleasure or enjoyment (voluptas), and to favor potency or efficiency in the sexual act.

After this introduction, the famous Dutch gynecologist says that a plentiful diet definitely assists sexual activity, while a frugal diet leads to the diminution and inhibition of this function. He stresses the value of meat, eggs (stimulant and restorative), milk-rice dishes, beetroots, carrots, turnips (all stewed in a milk sauce), crayfish soup (which he compares to bird's nest soup), celery, artichokes, truffles, saffron, cinnamon, pepper, and ginger.

Calves' brains, tastefully cooked, are a valuable sexual stimulant owing to their lecithin content.

Wilhelm Stekel, in *Impotence in the Male*, writes that, apart from organic disease involving impotence, a man only becomes old when he feels old, and only becomes impotent when he gives up his potency.

In men, the capacity for erection begins on the day of birth and extinguishes with death.

Fritz Kahn, M.D., in *Our Sex Life* tells us,

> The sex organs, like all other organs, require activity. As an organ built for reproduction, the sex organ demands realization of this productive activity... Evidently the law of exercise also holds true for the sex apparatus. It does not wear out and does not become exhausted. On the contrary, normal activity keeps the sex apparatus young and in good working order.

When not used, the sex apparatus atrophies!

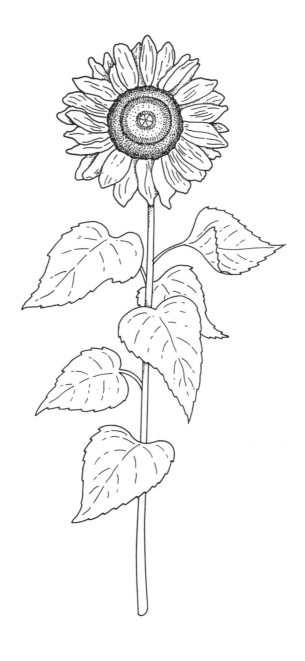

Sunflower

Not "For Men Only"

Women can have problems also!

They don't have to worry about erections, but they have many of the same problems with diet, neurotransmitters, vitamins, minerals, and more.

Some women say they seldom, if ever, experience an orgasm during their entired married life.

That could be because they can't relax enough.

There is a vicious cycle concerning relaxation and orgasm. When a woman does not reach a climax, she becomes tense and frustrated, which makes it harder and harder to have an orgasm.

Some difficulties in having an orgasm may originate in a lack of histamine release from the cells.

We've heard so much about antihistamines that we think of histamine as a "bad" thing. You can't turn on the TV or the radio without being offered this or that antihistamine to treat allergies and colds.

But histamines can shorten the time it takes to achieve orgasm!

And, for those women who can have a climax, it makes it even better.

According to Carl C. Pfeiffer, M.D., Ph.D., medical director of the Brain Bio Center of Princeton, New Jersey, the level of histamine in the cells can be raised—and with it the capacity to have an orgasm—by taking *concentrated virility foods* that contain pantothenic acid and rutin, or by taking these sex helpers in tablet form.

Doctor Pfeiffer explains that, in the past, low histamine levels in females caused women to be erroneously labeled as "frigid." But new research shows that females with high histamine levels can have repeated orgasms or orgasms with higher intensity and that continue far longer.

Rutin is a bioflavonoid frequently found with vitamin C in nature, while pantothenic acid is a member of the B complex family.

They may be purchased in health food or drugstores in tablet form.

Try taking pantothenic acid, fifty milligrams twice daily, and rutin fifty to one hundred milligrams three times a day.

Foods containing pantothenic acid are brewer's yeast, liver, peanuts, mushrooms, eggs, oatmeal, pecans, sardines, salmon, lentils, whole wheat, and brown rice.

However, it's difficult to get enough from food alone, and supplements may have to be used to obtain enough to change a lifetime of neglect.

Doctor Pfeiffer and other holistic physicians have turned to therapeutic nutrition in an effort to "cure" low histamine-caused lack of orgasm.

In addition to the use of pantothenic acid and rutin, the vitamin B3 member of the B-complex family in the form of niacin (niacinamide cannot be used) can be the most erotic vitamin for women.

Niacin produces a violent flush that resembles the flush of an excited woman.

If you're not aware that the flush will occur, you would be a bit frightened. The blood vessels closest to the skin widen and fill with blood. The skin becomes red and sensitive to the touch. The face, neck, head, arms, and chest heat up and a tingling sensation which begins in the ears moves down into the breasts, the torso, and eventually into the genital region.

If your timing is right the flush will intensify just as you're making love and will heighten the physical sensation.

If your orgasms have been light, the feeling will deepen and last longer.

Tell your partner what you have done so he will be able to watch the skin become pink and warm and contribute his touch to the touch of the *concentrated virility food.*

You can get niacin in a time-release form of supplement. This is a special formula that releases a bit of niacin at intervals during the day and evening. A little practice will enable you to know when to take it.

Or, you can take one hundred milligrams at the end of the meal three times a day. You may want to start off with fifty milligrams for a week or two and build up to one hundred.

You can try to add niacin-containing foods to your menu. Brown rice, peanuts, turkey or chicken, trout, halibut, swordfish, lamb, sesame seeds, pine nuts, buckwheat, barley, almonds, shrimp and haddock, contain fair amounts of the vitamin.

That's not the only vitamin that can be used to help bring back or bring on orgasm.

Vitamin B6 (pyridoxine) is involved in many metabolic processes and is important to the female orgasm. It may help you to reach a climax faster than you have in the past. It takes a woman longer to become aroused than a man, and longer for her to reach a climax. Vitamin B6 can therefore help bring the two of you closer to mutual ecstasy.

The body's sex hormones stimulate the basic parts of the sexual union, such as penile erection and vaginal lubrication. A shortage of hormones can have disastrous results. The endocrine system needs stimulation in order to do its job.

Vitamin B6 plays a direct role in the manufacture of sex hormones for both male and female.

Take B6, fifty milligrams two or three times a day with meals, or increase foods rich in B6 such as tuna, lima beans, navy beans, bananas, chestnuts, leeks, cauliflower, Brussels sprouts, sweet potatoes, raisins, turnip greens, spinach, and hazelnuts.

Or, do both!

Sex does not have to diminish with age. To the contrary, it can get better!

Armando deMoya, M.D., associate professor of obstetrics and gynecology at Georgetown and George Washington Universities, maintained in an article in *Harper's Bazaar*, September 1981 that for those who have always had good sex lives, there may be unexpected bonuses. And for those who have not been fulfilled, these years may bring new discoveries.

The older woman is free from the anxiety of conception and the energy-drain of children. She now has free time to devote to romance and sexual fulfillment.

If sex is not better and more frequent, she should look to her diet and to *concentrated virility foods.*

In addition to the mentioned nutrients, zinc and selenium (about fifteen milligrams of zinc daily and one hundred micrograms of selenium daily) have an influence on vaginal lubrication and the preservation of the elasticity of vaginal tissue.

Overcome sexual slowdown with stamina foods such as honeybee pollen, chromium, manganese, magnesium, vitamins A, E, C, D, plus the rest of the vitamins and minerals.

Try ginseng or dong-qui (available in health food stores). Try making tea from the herb damiana (formula in another part of the book) for increased sensitivity to oral or manual stimulation of the clitoris.

(Use damiana tea no more than three times a week. It will make you dream more vividly.)

If you are still in the throes of ending menopause, try using the combination of ginseng, vitamin E, and oil of evening primrose.

Ginseng can stimulate estrogen production, curb hot flashes and the loss of energy. Ginseng contains enzymes and chemicals that naturally stimulate a woman's body to produce more hormones. As a sexual supplement, two capsules (up to 650 milligrams) can be taken once or twice a day.

Vitamin E, up to four hundred International Units daily, plays an important role in keeping the genitals healthy and in keeping at a minimum damage to tender tissue from free radicals.

Oil of evening primrose is a natural oil extracted from the golden seeds of the plant. It is taken as a supplement in capsule form and, outside of mother's milk, is the only source of the essential fatty acids, linoleic and gamma-linoleic. These are the direct precursors for the body's production of prostaglandins. They are hormonelike substances that govern many actions and reactions, such as lubrication.

Take one 500 milligram capsule three times a day with meals.

Sex glands are also useful in rejuvenating waning sexual ability. Raw glandulars of ovarian and pituitary extract (combined) are available in health food stores.

If you take these glandulars, you can encourage the full activity of your own glands, encourage vital hormone production, and influence your own natural desire and arousal mechanisms.

Glandulars alone will not accomplish this, however. Good nutrition and the other sexual aids mentioned are required.

Slowing Down the Aging Process

No doubt, at forty-plus you are slowing down, but do you have to? What you will be, what you will do, how you will feel in ten, twenty, thirty years depends in large part on what you are eating now and what supplements you are taking. Senility, lack of sexual activity, or degenerative disease may not be as much a signal of age as it is of nutritive failure. So says Doctor Pearl Swanson, expert on the aging person, at the University of Iowa.

How do you begin to try to correct the situation? Start with your diet!

DMG. Dimethylglycine can help you get off the rocker and into the sack. The Moscow Clinical Hospital's Professor Yakov Shpirt says it is a powerful stimulant in the control of aging, and the *Medical Journal of Australia* claims that, with DMG, physical endurance has been shown to increase almost one hundred percent.

Citrus Fruits and Juices. Jethro Kloss says citrus fruits are life to the whole body. More than one hundred ailments are responsive to the healing powers of lemon. Citrus juices alkalize the system and contain vitamin A as the important Beta-carotene. They also contain amino acids and a large assortment of bioflavonoids. Fresh lemon juice has almost the same bacteriacidal action as garlic.

Iron and potassium are available in cherries and apricots and exert a favorable influence on the circulation.

Honey. Honey offers energy that is nonirritating and rapidly assimilated into the blood stream without having to be rerouted through the digestive system. This is completely different from refined sugar. Honey is an antistress food, and a mild stimulant to the heart. The world's oldest "young" people have been beekeepers who ate honey and pollen.

Pollen contains the B-complex vitamins, vitamin A, C, D, E, pantothenic acid, folic acid, and rutin. Prostatitis, sleeplessness, mental and physical anguish, forgetfulness, and a lack of concentration appear to respond favorably to a diet of pollen.

Vegetables. Eating quantities of vegetables, raw or steamed, can reduce or eliminate many of the infirmities associated with old age. Spinach can lower blood fat, while sorrel, kale, and cress are the richest natural sources of antiaging nutrients like sulfur, silicon, and ascorbic acid.

Nucleic Acids (RNA, DNA). Doctor Benjamin Frank, in his *No-Aging Diet* says that megadoses of foods rich in nucleic acids (spinach, beet greens, all sprouted seeds, brewer's yeast, sardines) will help make your skin more wrinkle-free in a matter of weeks.

Nuts, Seeds, Oils. Paavo Airola, in *Health Secrets from Europe*, says that essential fatty acids (EFA) help to keep cholesterol levels normal. Seeds are a source of complete protein, vitamins A, E, B complex, plus zinc, which has been linked directly to the health of the gonads and sex glands. It is also linked to the health of the prostate gland.

Antisenility seeds such as flaxseeds and linseed, two natural sources of linoleic acid, were thought of as "endurance foods" by the ancient Greeks and Romans.

Sprouts. Sprouts contain aspartic acid, an amino acid. The salts of aspartic acid have doubled the endurance levels of laboratory animals.

Herbs. Herbs for rejuvenation include alfalfa as a source of calcium, phosphorus, iron, potassium, magnesium, and vitamins A, D, E, and B-complex.

Comfrey is rich in a healing substance called allantoin, plus vitamin B12, calcium, ascorbic acid, potassium, and vitamin A.

Comfrey is rich in a healing substance called allantoin, plus vitamin B12, calcium, ascorbic acid, potassium, and vitamin A.

Other herbs include ginger, sarsaparilla, and dandelion. Look for the rejuvenating power of ginseng, gotu-kola, and others.

Seaweeds. Kelp is a safe source of iodine. It is a youth nutrient.

Needed by the thyroid gland for peak performance, it acts as a disinfectant to the blood system. A deficiency of iodine results in lethargy, inability to metabolize food properly, weight gain, and goiter. It is essential to the formation of thyroxin, a hormone which helps to balance estrogen levels in the body.

Other sea vegetables supply minerals like chromium (essential to glucose metabolism), zinc (for collagen strength and healthy skin), iron, potassium, copper, sulphur, zirconium, silicon (for skin elasticity), magnesium, and manganese. Trace minerals, important to maintaining healthy heart function, are also provided by seaweeds.

Look for nori, wakame, kombu, hiziki, arame, and dulse.

Fermented Foods. Fermented foods offer many antiaging benefits. These include foods such as yogurt and kefir (cultured lactic acid), sauerkraut, tofu, tempeh, and miso. Tempeh, a mild-flavored meat substitute made from fermented cracked soybean, is prepared without salt and is one of the richest sources of vitamin B12.

Tofu is low in saturated fat and calories, high in protein, and cholesterol-free! It is a food for health and long life. Both lecithin and linoleic acid are in tofu's unrefined oils. They help to emulsify and eliminate cholesterol deposits that have accumulated in the blood stream and in vital organs. By using tofu instead of meat, you can reduce cholesterol intake and help to remove it from the body.

Miso is a source of energy and stamina. It is salty, and can substitute for table salt in many dishes.

Soy Lecithin. Doctor Richard Wurtman in *Psychology Today* said that eating lecithin may one day combat the forgetfulness of old age. The simple reason is that lecithin breaks down into choline in the body, and choline is one of the raw materials to make acetylcholine, the memory neurotransmitter!

Tests show that giving people choline increases their memory and learning ability. In other words, it makes them smarter. These are the findings of Doctor Christian Gillin, a researcher and official at the National Institute of Mental Health in Bethesda, Maryland.

Vitamins and Minerals. All vitamins and minerals are important to help keep a person healthy and to ensure a long life, but some are more important than others.

Vitamin C is needed in larger quantities as people grow older. It goes a long way to help prop up sagging vigor. The Russians believe it is the fountain of youth, according to Paavo Airola.

Adequate supplies of vitamin A help maintain normal growth and bone development, healthy skin and nails, good vision, and help keep protective sheathing around the nerves intact. Vitamin A also aids the respiratory system, and fights infection and allergy.

There is hardly any function in the body that doesn't involve the B-complex family of vitamins. While these vitamins may be plentiful in foods, older people may fail to absorb them properly, warns Doctor H. L. Newbold. Vitamin B1 aids carbohydrate metabolism, growth, good digestion, and nerve function. The vitamin B2 is essential for a healthy respiratory system and for healthy skin and eye tissue.

Vitamin E is an incredible substance. A deficiency of vitamin E resembles the effect of radiation damage and contributes to the damage due to old age, according to Doctor William A. Pryor of Louisiana State University.

Research shows that vitamin E is a conditioner for the skin and appears to hold off the premature effects of aging.

Minerals are of an importance equal to that of vitamins. Older people should increase their use of selenium, calcium, zinc, and magnesium.

Doctor Gerhard Schrauzer, professor of chemistry at the University of California, San Diego, says that if Americans increased their intake of selenium, the death rates in the United States from common types of cancer would drop dramatically. In countries where the selenium intake is higher in the diet, the deaths from cancer are one-third the rate of those in the United States. The average American diet contains between fifty and one hundred fifty micrograms of selenium, while it is estimated that two hundred to three hundred micrograms are needed.

Selenium, recognized in 1975 as an essential nutrient in human nutrition, is found in whole grains, seafood, egg yolk, milk, garlic, and nutritional yeast.

Zinc is a constituent of nearly one hundred human enzymes involved in major metabolic processes. It helps to get vitamin A out of storage in the liver. Without an adequate supply of zinc, you can be deficient in vitamin A, no matter how much you take. Zinc is needed for a good complexion and for decay-free teeth. A deficiency of zinc can lead to joint pains and a poor immune response to invading bacteria and viruses.

Calcium is the main mineral needed after age forty. It builds and maintains bone structure, heals wounds, improves nerves, counteracts acidity, improves muscle function, ensures proper blood clotting, and gives vitality and endurance.

Magnesium is an important catalyst in many enzyme reactions, especially those concerned with energy. It helps the body utilize the B-complex vitamins and vitamin E, fats, calcium, and other material needed for healthy muscles and bones. It is essential to the acid-alkaline balance and for lecithin production within the body. It is a natural tranquilizer and helps prevent the build up of cholesterol.

Garlic and Onions. Early in history a Greek physician, Dioscordes, said that eating two cloves of garlic a day for one month will kill off harmful intestinal bacteria and promote the growth of health-boosting bacteria.

For a cold, take a garlic clove every two hours with a cup of yarrow tea.

Garlic is used to treat high and low blood pressure and dyspepsia (gas).

According to *Science News*, East Texas State University scientists say the onion may be an agent to lower blood pressure. Onion extract injected into rats successfully lowered their pressure!

The leading causes of death in the United States are heart disease, cancer, accidents, cerebrovascular disease, chronic liver diseases, pneumonia, and influenza.

Small wonder that antiaging substances, which might help

prevent or curb the debilitating effects of these killers, are so sought after!

The following is a brief list of some of the antiaging nutrients that so many books have been written about. It is a primer so that you will be able to familiarize yourself with the various categories and examples of substances currently being incorporated into life-extension programs. You owe it to yourself to be aware of the exciting developments in optimizing human intelligence, health, and longevity through dietary means.

Antioxidants. Lecithin, L-cysteine, L-methionine, PABA, selenium, glutathione, vitamins A, B1, C, and E.

Antistress. Calcium, biotin, folic acid, magnesium, niacin, ginseng, PABA, L-tryptophan, vitamins B1, B2, B5, B6, and C.

Blood Nourishers. Folic acid, ginseng, and iron.

Brain-fuction Enhancers. Choline, lecithin, manganese, niacin, inositol, zinc, vitamin B6, L-phenylalanine, L-tyrosine, and L-tryptophan.

Cardiac Protectors. Chromium, inositol, magnesium, manganese, niacin, selenium, linoleic and linolenic acids, zinc, vitamins A, E, and C.

Detoxifying Agents. Cysteine, ginseng, methionine, SOD, glutathione, gotu-kola, selenium, and vitamin C.

DNA Repair Aids. Biotin, choline, chromium, cysteine, orotic acid, molybdenum, nucleic acids, zinc, manganese, methionine, vitamins B1, B6, B2, B5, C, and E.

Immune-system Strengtheners. Selenium, zinc, arginine, ornithine, vitamins C and E.

Membrane Stabilizers. Manganese, nucleic acids, vitamins A, B1 and E.

Protein-synthesis Factors. Biotin, chromium, cysteine, folic acid, nucleic acid, zinc, methionine, vitamins B3, B5, B6, and C.

Lipofuscin Controllers. Magnesium orotate, papain, bromelain, kawain from the kava-kava plant (pipe methysticum).

Antiaging Skin Factors. Cysteine, all of the vitamins and minerals, and papain.

Sex-drive Enhancers. All of the items in this book!

How do you calculate a person's true age?

Instead of going only by the year of birth, using the following to determine true age: biological age, physiological age, pathological age, sexual age, emotional age, motivational age.

As you can see, age is a relative thing. People can do many things to lower one or all of their "ages." According to Doctor Linus Pauling, increasing the intake of vitamin C to eight or ten grams a day (a very large dose) may increase lifespan by as much as twenty-four years.

Doctor Benjamin Frank believed that the nucleic acids DNA and RNA, either from food or supplements or both, could be of great benefit to the cells in retarding age. Researchers report that nucleic acids are effective antioxidants, and reduce the formation of free radicals, which can cause great damage within the body.

Doctor Isaac Asimov believes that a dominant factor in aging is the radiation which bombards our cells, both from outer space and from radioactive elements within the body.

Some of the policing agents which help protect the cell from breakdown are vitamin C, vitamin A, vitamin E, selenium, iodine, zinc, and nucleic acids.

Doctor Ana Aslan in Rumania has made many claims for Gerovital H 3, a buffered form of procaine. The principal response to her treatment seems to be an elevated feeling of well-being. It is held that Gerovital reduces depression, smoothes wrinkles, improves memory, and increases energy.

Doctor Aslan has achieved worldwide prominence and has treated many famous people, including one U. S. President. The scientists believe that the procaine blocks monamine exidates (MAO). High levels of MAO tend to induce depression. Accordingly, in reducing the level of MAO, procaine may tend to create a sense of well-being that promotes better health.

Psychiatrist L. J. Kotkas of Alberta, Canada, agrees that any agent that reduces stress, reduces depression, or promotes a sense of well-being—if it is not a drug that is toxic to the body or the mind—is of great benefit to the general health.

There have been many different theories and techniques applied to regeneration. The most spectacular approach was that of cell injections by Doctor Paul Niehans of Switzerland. His technique was to determine the particular organ in the body that needed regeneration and then to inject his patient with the fetal cells of that organ, taken from an animal. Many of the most famous people of the world went to his clinic and reported feeling better. He treated Winston Churchill, Conrad Adenauer, Charles de Gaulle, King George VI, Pope Pius XII, the Duke of Windsor, Bernard Baruch, Bob Cummings, Charlie Chaplin, Ann Miller, and Gloria Swanson.

His successor, Doctor Walter Michel, still carries on with the theory and treatment at a clinic near Lausanne, Switzerland.

The most plausible explanation of fresh cell therapy is offered by Doctor Hans J. Kugler in his book *Slowing Down The Aging Process*. He says that after the injection, the entire cell disintegrates, making all of the basic undamaged cell products available for regeneration of older cells. Doctor Kugler believes that fresh cell injection is more effective than oral ingestion of nucleic acids, although he does believe that Doctor Benjamin S. Frank's claims regarding the benefits of oral ingestion of nucleic acids are valid.

Pantothenic acid is one of the favorites of Doctor Roger Williams, who first discovered this essential nutrient. He believes it prevents a host of bodily ailments and clearly extends the life span.

He reported in his book, *Nutrition Against Disease*, that mice whose diet contained extra pantothenic acid lived about nineteen percent longer than those who did not. He points out that the worker bee, which does not get any royal jelly, lives only a few weeks during the summer. On the other hand, the queen bee, which eats royal jelly rich in pantothenic acid, may live as long as six to eight years!

Body cells are constantly being worn out and replaced. If the raw materials are available to the body, better cells can replace worn out cells and good health can blossom where poor health existed before. We know that cellular breakdown causes aging and that the impairment of our life systems is the result of cellular breakdown. We can discourage this process by means of particular nutrients.

As Ashley Montague, anthropologist and author, has said, "One should die young as late as possible."

To which I say, "Amen."

Scientists are not sitting with their hands under their posteriors, since they understand that *they* age also. Science has come up with a biochemical marvel that's a triple treat against the aging process: a nutritional substance produced in the body is now available as a supplement. It is an amino acid compound of L-cysteine, L-glutamic acid, and glycine. Chemically it is called glutathione.

The work was first revealed in articles by Dwight Kalita, Ph.D., research director for the Huxley Institute of Biosocial Research, and Steve Blechman, research scientist. Chemically, glutathione is a sulfur amino acid tripeptide, with a long list of its published credits:

- Serves as an antitumor agent
- Detoxifies heavy metals
- Helps to treat liver and blood disorders
- Plays an important role in retarding the aging process and strengthening the immune system
- Aids in the treatment of allergies, cataracts, diabetes, and arthritis
- Accelerates respiration in the brain
- Protects against cigarette smoke and the effects of alcohol

In February of 1982 a research paper was presented to the New York Academy of Sciences stating that oral doses of glutathione could be absorbed by the intestinal tract.

A study conducted at the University of Louisville School of Medicine demonstrated that the *glutathione content in red blood cells* of research animals *decreased with advancing age.*

Doctor George Hazleton, involved in the study, writes, "The present evidence suggests that a low glutathione content may be a general phenomenon of all aging tissue and not restricted to a few specialized tissues."

According to another study, glutathione is involved in our body's defense system. Gareth Green of Harvard Medical School says that glutathione is intimately related to the phagocytic activity of certain lung cells. Phagocytes help to catch and destroy harmful bacteria.

Recent experiments by reputable scientists suggest that antioxidants such as vitamin C, vitamin E, Beta-carotene, and the amino acids L-cysteine and glutathione can acutally inhibit carcinogenesis (the onset of cancer) when the antioxidants are administered prior to or at the same time as the carcinogens.

All of this news is extremely interesting, but we must always keep in mind that no one specific chemical normally occurring within the human body "cures" anything by itself. These chemicals or substances are team players; that is, they must work together for the benefit of the whole body. Drugs, on the other hand, act singularly and radically, and they alter the body's machinery. But nutrients are not drugs, because they act constructively as building blocks of life and optimum health. Nutrients take time to act because they work from the basic cell level outward, using the body's systems to promote body health.

There is no overnight success when you resort to nutritional help, but rather a gradual building of strength and health that will not leave and will not have disastrous side effects.

You and Your Prostate Gland

One out of every four men past age forty has a problem with the prostate gland.

The symptoms are painful or difficult urination; urine retention; infection or tenderness; frequent urination—even disturbing sleep.

As men grow older, into their sixties and seventies, the chance of having a problem with this gland becomes even stronger.

What is the prostate gland?

What does it do?

Why does it give almost everybody a little trouble and some people a lot of trouble?

Does it interfere with having sex, and are there special *concentrated virility foods* that can help?

The prostate is a walnut-sized gland located near the opening of the male bladder. It lies around the urethra, the tube which drains the bladder.

If the gland is enlarged or swollen, it puts pressure on the urethra and can interfere with the flow of urine.

Of Mice and Men and Cancer

When it comes to cancer of the prostate, many studies have been done on mice and men. Several nutritional factors can influence the course of prostate cancer.

One epodemiological study done in Japan strongly suggests that *concentrated virility foods*, such as green and yellow vegetables, make healthier prostates.

This was not a small study.

One hundred thousand men participated.

It was discovered that a *high intake of green and yellow vegetables* was correlated with a *low mortality rate* from prostate cancer.

Japanese men who were protected from cancer ate twice as many green and yellow vegetables as are found in the typical American diet.

The risk of prostate cancer in Americans is five to six times higher than it is to the Japanese.

One of the suggested answers is the presence of Beta-carotene in the vegetables.

Vitamin A is found in animal tissue, where it is known as vitamin A, or in vegetable tissue, where it is known as Beta-carotene.

Beta-carotene is vegetable vitamin A. That is, it is two molecules of vitamin A linked together. If the body needs vitamin A, it cuts the linkage by use of a special enzyme and releases the vitamin to do its job. If it doesn't happen to need any vitamin A at the time it leaves it whole.

That's the reason you cannot overdose on Beta-carotene (or vegetable vitamin A).

NOTE: Diabetics, in some cases, cannot cut the linkage to release the vitamin A and therefore must use preformed vitamin A from fish liver oil.

Even mice need vitamin A to protect their prostate glands. Tests show that mice given vitamin A can reverse the precancerous condition of their prostate glands.

Female mice do not have a prostate gland, but vitamin A helped protect them from cervical cancer.

Concentrated virility foods can help you prevent cancer both in your sexual glands and in your sexual organs.

To understand the protection effect, you must first understand the development of cancer as it is understood.

Briefly, cancer is a two-stage process.

The first is the initiation stage, during which there are some abnormal changes in the cell. At this point there may be a few cancerous cells present.

What happens during the next stage may determine whether or not you develop cancer. The second stage can last for thirty years or more. It's called the promotional stage.

Vitamin A apparently blocks the progression of cancer during the promotional stage.

On the other hand, an excessive consumption of dietary fat can hasten the development of certain cancers (prostate, breast, uterus, colon, and rectal).

The dosage of vitamin A or Beta-carotene, from both foods and supplements, should be about 20,000 International Units a day.

Consider the following foods and their vitamin A content:

1 raw carrot—5,000 IU
1 cup asparagus—1,500 IU
1 stalk broccoli—3,500 IU
5 ounces sweet potato—15,000 IU
1 raw tomato—1,800 IU
1 cup cooked butternut squash—13,000 IU

1 cup carrots and peas—15,000 IU
2 to 3 medium apricots—2,700 IU
¼ cantaloupe—3,500 IU
½ mango—4,800 IU
⅓ papaya—1,750 IU

You can see why a diet which includes yellow and green foods can be a source of *concentrated virility foods* which protect your sexy parts.

The main function of the prostate gland is to produce fluids for the male sperm. It's in the prostate that the *vas diferens,* the tube that transports sperm from the testicles, connects to the urethra. From there the urethra goes out through the penis to deliver either urine or sperm, depending on the occasion.

Under normal circumstances you don't even know the prostate is there. It does its job and you enjoy its efforts. However, because it is placed in such a strategic spot, if there is trouble you get to know about it rapidly.

If if is enlarged or infected, you have trouble peeing!

If it is enlarged or infected, intercourse can be a pain.

The over-forty crowd can be troubled by a condition known as benign prostatic hypertrophy (BPH). It's a scary combination of words, but all it means is that the prostate is enlarged but not cancerous.

By age sixty, nearly half of adult males have some form of BPH.

Why do we have a gland that can get into so much trouble?

Well, we need it!

It supplies half the ejaculate, and its share is rich in the trace mineral zinc, one of the *concentrated virility foods.* The prostate contains the highest concentration of zinc in the whole body. Next highest concentration is in the eyes.

Do you remember that far back when the "old wives' tale" said if you masturbate too much you'll go blind?

You do lose a lot of zinc each time you ejaculate; that's why a zinc supplement is recommended for every male who wants to remain virile and still play gin rummy with the boys!

Benign prostatic hypertrophy can start with the urine stream weakening a little. Then you find you have to get up during the night to go to the bathroom. Usually there's no pain, but the condition begins to get worse, so you go to the doctor. He puts on a rubber glove, reaches for the jar of Vaseline petroleum jelly and examines you rectally. It's no fun, but it's the only way to really confirm the diagnosis.

Mild BPH can be treated nutritionally and through some dietary changes: beer will have to go, and cut down on any alcoholic beverage. No more chili peppers, and have your pizza without pepperoni. Cut back on coffee and tea, even the decaffeinated kind. Drink a lot of water daily, six to ten glasses a day, and pee as frequently as the urge strikes you! You don't want to distend your bladder.

To treat the condition nutritionally is to understand the gland better. The prostate is made up of a specialized arrangement of proteins, fats, and minerals. Most of the important functions in the body are the result of hormonal activity. To make hormones, certain substances are required as raw material. Among them are fatty acids.

Some doctors have found that the addition of foods high in fatty acids have a rejuvenating effect on the prostate gland, often keeping it functional throughout your entire life.

W. L. Cooper, M.D., of Los Angeles treated nineteen prostate patients with unsaturated fatty acids. He had the following results:

- Less residual urine
- Increased sexual libido
- Decreased leg pains
- Decreased fatigue
- Dribbling eliminated in eighteen cases
- Force of urinary stream increased
- Gland size reduced

Doctor Cooper put his patients on a daily dosage of six 5-grain tablets of vitamin F complex, a concentrate containing linoleic, linolenic, and arachidonic acids. Each tablet had a total of ten milligrams of these unsaturated fatty acids.

This dose was given for a period of three days to produce systemic saturation; it was then reduced to four tablets daily for several weeks; finally a maintenance dose of one or two tablets was to be taken daily.

The use of unsaturated fatty acids is not new to folk medicine. Pumpkin seeds have always been valued as a treatment for prostate problems.

Primitive people believed that "like treats like," and, since the seed of the plant is akin to the semen in men, they believed that eating seeds could be of help to the sex organs. Turns out that they were right!

Maybe they didn't know about hormones, minerals, and fatty acids, but the men of Bulgaria, the Ukraine, Turkey, and other countries ate a handful of pumpkin seeds every day to ensure their vitality.

Benjamin F. Sievem, M.D., of Boston wrote that vitamins and hormones combine forces to create or restore health. Infection, emotional upset, and mechanical interference with nutritional intake all prevent a healthy state.

When he studied two hundred cases of BPH, Doctor Sievem found that sixty percent were caused by infection accompanied by nutritional deficiency. With the use of nutrition, Dr. Sievem was able to avoid surgery in seventy percent of his patients.

Some specific *concentrated virility foods* which act to protect the prostate are:

Vitamin A—This vitamin is needed for the reasons already talked about and because it's used by mucous membrane to fight infection. Without a constant supply to bathe the tissues, the tiny hairs called cilia, which sweep germ and extraneous material out of the body, atrophy and are replaced by keratin. Keratin is a horny tissue which can crack easily and expose the inner cells to invasion by bacteria. Vitamin A is also needed as a lubricant inducer.

Vitamin C — This vitamin cannot be manufactured in the body and must be obtained from food or supplements every day. It acts as a superantibiotic, cleansing the urinary tract and keeping free radicals from damaging prostate tissue.

Clorophyll — This is the material that makes green plants green. It has been called "plant blood," since its composition and function are so much like our human blood. It is a source of fat-soluble vitamins and essential fatty acids. It also acts to combat infection and to help heal mucous membrane.

Zinc — When a gland is found to be diseased it is also found to be deficient in zinc. Therefore, a daily supply of zinc is healing and protective. Zinc and vitamin C act in unison to help heal an enlarged gland. Oysters have been used for centuries as an aphrodisiac and as a cure for sexual problems. They were first used because of the "like-cures-like" concept. Oysters look like testicles, so they must be good for them. Actually, oysters happen to be the richest natural source of zinc!

All glands are made up of amino acids in selected ratios. Kidneys need certain amino acids, the spleen needs different amino acids, and the prostate requires a specific combination.

According to Kurt W. Donsbach, Ph.D., the body may heal itself from BPH.

Such healing requires a diet of health-giving meals of fresh vegetables, fresh fruit, whole grains, fish, fowl, and selected dairy products; and the avoidance of processed grains, sugar, alcohol, coffee, and tea (except for herb tea).

Doctor Donsbach suggests a handful of pumpkin seeds daily.

He also suggests the following nutritional formula taken daily, one tablet three times a day with meals. Daily total as follows:

Vitamin A	25,000 IU
Vitamin C	1,000 milligrams
Zinc	30 milligrams
Chlorophyll	70 milligrams
Glycine	470 milligrams
Alanine	70 milligrams
Glutamic Acid	70 milligrams
Prostate Extract	100 milligrams

You don't have to hunt around to make your own formula, since it is available in health food stores.

Because the amounts of the nutrients exceed the RDA, you might want to check with your physician before beginning the routine.

Also, look around for pumpkin seed oil. A lot of people with tooth problems may have difficulty in chewing a handful of seeds a day. Pumpkin seed oil comes in capsules and will offer all of the nutrients found in the seeds, which benefit the body and the prostate gland.

I can't stress the use of zinc too much.

Within the prostate there is a substance known as "prostatic antibacterial factor," which is very rich in zinc. It looks like the ability of this factor to kill off bacteria is related to the amount of zinc present in the prostatic fluid. Researchers now think that this factor may serve as a natural defense system against all kinds of prostate torture.

A decreased zinc content in the prostatic fluid may be a prelude to bacterial invasion rather than the effect of bacterial growth.

Impotence is fairly common among men with kidney disease who are being treated by dialysis.

When zinc is added to the dialysis solution (as ordered by the doctor) there is a striking improvement in potency and an increase in testosterone levels as well. It can also occur with oral zinc supplementation.

Zinc is great for your love life.

Alcohol and coffee hinder absorption of zinc and cause an increase in zinc loss.

A word to the wise!

Keep 'Em Swimming

You don't want any more kids.

Your wife is past the child-bearing stage.

Why do you need to keep your sperm healthy and swimming?

Because nature responds to ripe conditions!

Remember your first car and a full tank of gas; it couldn't just sit there, it had to do something, go somewhere.

Same thing with a full testicle of sperm. They want to do something, go somewhere. So, they urge you to get it on!

Nobody says sex equals pregnancy, so if you keep away from the nubile young thing in the next apartment and spend your sperm at home, free-swimming, healthy sperm will keep your sex life on the top burner.

Many *concentrated virility foods* are involved in sperm production and sperm health. Zinc, vitamin A, and selenium are among them.

Sperm are born in the testicles and, when they are mature enough, migrate to the prostate where they are "energized" for their final destination.

Testicles must have adequate amounts of vitamin A and zinc, or hormone production falls and sperm production is lowered or stopped altogether.

If this happens, the sex drive is decreased as well.

A lack of zinc interferes with the sperm's motility. They swim by waving a "tail" back and forth, a little like a tadpole whipping its way through the water. If there's not enough of this mineral, the tail is shortened and the sperm has to do the breast stroke!

Anything that interferes with good nutrition interferes with sperm production.

Alcohol interferes with vitamin A metabolism in the blood stream. Alcohol is a poison, so the body tries to get rid of it as quickly as possible. It has to be metabolized by the liver. But, the same process that gets rid of alcohol is used to release vitamin A. The body has the choice of getting rid of the alcohol or releasing vitamin A. It must choose to get rid of the alcohol. Vitamin A suffers and so does sperm production, so, alchohol can make you less sexy!

It also interferes with zinc.

Alcohol is damaging to the liver. Most people know that, but few people know that it is also damaging to the testicles. Since both the liver and the testicles are involved in hormone production, the ultimate result can be a disaster.

Damaged testicles will interfere with libido, will interfere with sexual prowess and enjoyment.

Excessive alcohol can cause your testicles to atrophy.

You can become sterile and impotent.

Sperm production also needs the B vitamins!

A deficiency of the B vitamins impairs the activity of the pituitary gland, which, in turn, adversely affects the testicles.

Too little male hormone is produced.

You can become deficient in the B vitamins in times of stress or if you are too tense for long periods of time.

Relax with the amino acid L-tryptophan (two hundred fifty milligrams during the day) and take a B-50 tablet of B complex twice a day. Both are available at the health food store, just ask for them.

Sugar, alcohol, and caffeine help to rob your body of the B-complex family of vitamins.

Add B-rich foods to your menu: eggs, fish, lean meats, legumes (dried peas, beans, and lentils), liver, milk, poultry, nuts, and brewer's yeast.

Cigarettes don't help sperm either!

If you smoke, your sperm, if you have any, are likely to be poor swimmers, and deformed as well.

Selenium, the *concentrated virility food*, is also necessary for active sperm. It protects the testicles against damage from heavy metals such as cadmium. It acts as an antioxidant in the body to protect tender tissues from hazardous interaction with oxidants like cadmium, mercury, lead, and other pollutants.

It is also a barrier against the action of peroxides and other free radicals which hasten the aging process.

You need a battery of antioxidants on your side if you want to live a long time and remain sexually active.

Other major antioxidants include vitamin C, vitamin E, the B vitamins, zinc, vitamin A, and the two sulfur-amino acids L-cysteine and L-methionine.

Because sperm are very rich in phospholipids, which contain fatty acids, they are highly susceptible to lipid peroxides. These are toxic to sperm, causing them to clump together and to quit swimming. Vitamin E and vitamin C are particularly helpful to guard against the peroxides and to restore normal motility.

Other minerals which lend their support to sperm production are calcium, manganese, and magnesium.

A good therapeutic vitamin-mineral formula will include all of these nutrients. Take one tablet twice a day with meals.

Vitamin C, in particular, improves sperm motility. This may be due to its antioxidant power, as it intervenes with free radicals, helping to inactivate them. Because oxidant stress is very harmful to the gonads, vitamin C may also be protective against cancer as well.

The fall of the Roman Empire has been blamed on lead poisoning. The early Romans ate most of their meals from lead dishes, they cooked in lead pots, and drank from lead cups. This, it is suspected, caused infertility.

Studies have shown that in the last twenty-five years, sperm density in the United States has declined appreciably. This could be the result of heavy metal pollutants in our environment, such as lead, cadmium, and mercury. So, eat wholesome food, wash your fruits and vegetables well before you eat them, take vitamins and antioxidants regularly, and make sure that your vitamin formula includes A, C, E, Beta-carotene, zinc, selenium, and the B complex.

Vitamins and Minerals

If you haven't figured it out by now, then it's time to tell you! The love-power of all foods, eaten singly or combined, depends on the known and unknown nutritional factors the foods contain.

Supplements are strongly recommended for two reasons. One, they help to manipulate the quantity and quality of the nutrients your body needs to enjoy all of the benefits of sex. Two, we can't be sure the nutrients that *should* be in the food actually *are* there. With all of the problems in getting food from the ground to the table, we just don't know if the vitamins and minerals are really in the food we eat. Also, since so many nutrients are leached from the land, the food may not have had any to absorb during its growing season. So, the best insurance is a good health food or drugstore.

Vitamins and minerals are usually not harmful if you use common sense in picking the amounts that will benefit you. There may be a problem with the oil-soluble vitamins A and D. Try to keep your vitamin A intake at about 20,000 IU a day, and your vitamin D content at about 400 IU a day. The water-soluble vitamins, vitamin C and the entire B complex are usually not dangerous unless you go hog-wild and eat the entire bottle at one sitting. It won't kill you, but you might get a stomach ache.

Vitamins, minerals, and diet can revitalize and prolong your sexual activity and your sexual life. You owe it to yourself to learn as much as you can about how these valuable elements can help you.

Vitamin A

This vitamin is the protector of your mucous membrane, wherever it is in the body. That includes the mouth, nose, eyes, stomach and intestines, genitourinary tract, lungs, and so on. Without enough vitamin A, sexual activity will diminish or even vanish altogether. The mucous-secreting cells stop doing their job, and the surrounding tissue can become dry and scaly and completely lack lubrication. If the condition continues long enough, keratinization sets in and the tissue becomes like horn. Keratin is a normal protein of hair and nails, but you don't want it on your tender tissues.

The tissue can waste away and become susceptible to bacterial infection. Vitamin A, by maintaining a healthy epithelium, can also interrupt the process by which some cancers are formed.

Good sources of vitamin A include whole milk and yellow and dark green vegetables, such as carrots, pumpkins, squash, sweet potatoes, broccoli, peas, collard greens, endive, kale, peppers, spinach, turnip greens.

Vitamin A is also obtained from orange fruits such as apricots, cantaloupe, papaya, peaches. Other sources are watermelon and cherries.

Liver is also a good source of vitamin A, since a three-ounce serving contains about 45,000 IU.

Butter, fish oil, and egg yolk all contribute vitamin A to the diet, while small amounts can be found in corn, green beans, beets, cabbage, cauliflower, onions, parsnips, apples, cranberries, dates, grapefruit, pears, strawberries, and pineapple.

Too small a vitamin A intake increases susceptibility to cancer. Green and yellow vegetables help make a healthier prostate gland. As we have said previously, Japanese men eat twice as many green and yellow vegetables as do American men, and the incidence of prostate cancer shows it. This cancer is five to six times higher among American whites than it is among the Japanese. American blacks, on the other hand, have twice the risk as American whites!

Vitamin A is also needed for the production of all sex hormones.

Can you get too much of a good thing? It's hard, but some people have been known to eat so many foods that were in the golden-yellow class that their skin began to take on an orange appearance. It has happened, but if it does, just cut down on the amount of foods containing vitamin A. The color will fade away.

The recommended daily allowance for vitamin A is five thousand IU a day. Most nutritionists think the RDA is too low, and they take twenty thousand to twenty-five thousand IU daily. As with all supplements, do not restrict your intake to just one vitamin. You need them all.

In 1982 a Gallup Poll showed that about one-third of all Americans used some form of nutritional supplement on a regular basis. In 1985 another poll showed that people who exercised as a part of an overall health strategy were even more likely to use supplements.

People who use supplements also have more trust in their own ability to take care of their own problems and have developed more of a medical self-reliance than other people.

That's you, after you finish this book!

It's difficult to get enough nutrients without using some supplements. There are many reasons for this, and they apply to all of us, especially as we advance in years.

- We all have unique genetic nutritional requirements and these can be affected by drugs, hormones, disease, stress, surgery, and emotional and behavioral factors.
- We don't eat a "balanced" diet because we are guided by what we like best or what is convenient.
- Foods vary in nutritional content due to the soil on which the food was grown. Depleted soil yields depleted foods.
- Dieting makes it very difficult to get the necessary nutrients.

• Pollutants in our food, water, and air burden our systems and our immune defenses beyond belief, requiring supplements to keep us healthy.

Michael Colgan, Ph.D., in his book, *Your Personal Vitamin Profile*, has given his views on the amounts of vitamins and minerals that are needed on a daily basis. His recommendations and those of other nutritionists will be included in this chapter to illustrate the sameness and the differences in daily allowances.

Doctor Colgan's RDAs

Nutrient	Recommended daily allowance
Vitamin A	5,000-30,000 IU
Vitamin B1	2-75 mg
Vitamin B2	2-55 mg
Vitamin B3	20-150 mg
Vitamin B5	10-50 mg
Vitamin B6	10-75 mg
Vitamin B12	10-100 mg
Folic acid	0.5-2 mg
Biotin	2-5 mg
Inositol	100-500 mg
Para-aminobenzoic acid	50-100 mg
Choline	100-300 mg
Vitamin C	300-2,000 mg
Vitamin D	400-4,000 IU
Vitamin E	50-600 IU
Zinc	15-50 mg
Iron	20-30 mg
Calcium	800-1,200 mg
Magnesium	400-1,000 mg
Manganese	10-50 mg
Phosphorus	800-1,500 mg
Potassium	1,000-3,500 mg
Copper	0.5-2 mg
Molybdenum	10-150 mcg
Chromium	2-5 mg
Selenium	50-100 mcg

Doctor Colgan's formula illustrates the number of vitamins and minerals that are basic to good health. Most people find it easiest to take the almost thirty basic nutrients in the form of a multivitamin and mineral tablet or capsule. Doctor Colgan's concept of what quantities are needed is just one expert's opinion.

A good, basic formula is the start of a nutritional campaign to restore good health. Once that has begun, it may be necessary to add other nutrients or to add more of some of the nutrients you are taking in your multiple formula. For example, you may want to take the water-soluble vitamins (B complex and C) more than once a day, because they are usually lost in the urine. Or there may be a dependency situation (frequent colds or infections) that requires using high doses of vitamin C three times a day.

Other nutrients may be needed, such as superoxide dismutaste, octacosanol, glutathione peroxidase, oil of evening primrose, max EPA, garlic extract, onion extract, alfalfa tablets, amino acids (L-phenylalanine, L-tyrosine, L-cysteine, L-glutamine, L-tryptophan), herbs such as ginseng or gotu-kola. *You* are inside your body, and only you can decide on quantities and how to take them.

This book and others offer information, nutrition tips, food for your sex survival and foods for your immunological system. Once you have all of the available information, you have to begin to use what you have learned.

It's really a course in self-defense. Look at these statistics gathered by the Office of Technology Assessment:

- Seventy percent of deaths are caused by diseases linked to diet, including high levels of fat, sugar, and salt.
- Autopsies of young soldiers who died in World War I rarely showed signs of arteriosclerosis (*Journal of the American Medical Association*); however, autopsies of American youths who died in Vietnam showed that it was rare to find a young soldier who *did not* have arteriosclerosic disease.
- One out of every five children born in the United States is afflicted with hyperactivity or brain damage, or has a learning disability.

- In the 1980s, almost eighty percent of our food is processed. Compare that to 1910, when only ten percent was processed.
- Frozen vegetables can have one hundred percent more salt than fresh vegetables.
- The use of food coloring increased 995 percent between 1940 and 1976.
- A meal of a hamburger, french fries, and a milkshake at a fast food center contains twenty-two additives with at least twelve of them shown to be reasonably toxic.
- Fifty percent of the average American's diet calories come from refined sugar and refined carbohydrates.
- On the average, we consume nine pounds of additives each year. These are substances the body was not programmed to ingest or to digest, substances the caveman never came across and the body never learned how to handle.
- The United States recommended daily allowance (RDA) of vitamin A for pigs is two hundred percent greater than for humans. The RDA of vitamin A for dogs is three hundred percent greater than for humans. It appears the government looks out for pigs and dogs, and lets us try to take care of ourselves — but not by giving us all of the necessary information!

Seniors have some unique nutritional requirements because the efficiency of certain organs may have gone down or some medicines interfere with nutritional uptake. According to Doctor Jeffrey Blumberg, a pharmacologist and assistant director of the U. S. Department of Agriculture's Human Nutrition Research Center of Aging at Tufts University in Boston, there is impaired absorption of such nutrients as folic acid, B1 and B2. The elderly may need more nutrients than when they were younger, according to the doctor. Caloric intake can be reduced because of reduced activity, but the nutritional requirements remain the same or are increased. Perhaps if the elderly got more of certain nutrients, the aging process would slow down!

H. W. Holderby, M.D., refers to circulation problems that interefere with many activities, including sex. Increased cholesterol or tryglycerides, either or both, leads to the formation of plaques in the arteries and eventually to poor blood transport of nutrients and even to blockage.

Doctor Holderby recommends decreasing the amount of fat in the diet to twenty percent, substituting vegetable oils for animal fats, elminating fried foods, salty foods, alcohol, sugar, and sweets. He suggests eating whole grains (oatmeal, brown rice), legumes (peas, beans, lentils), potatoes with their skins, skim or other low-fat milk.

His supplement recommendations for elevated cholesterol are as follows:

Vitamin C	1,000 to 3,000 mg daily
Selenium	200 to 300 mcg daily
Vitamin E	400 IU daily and increase if the cholesterol level increases
Guargum	5 to 10 grams a day
Oatmeal	6 tablespoons a day
Garlic	2 capsules three times a day
Chromium	200 to 300 mcg daily
GLA or oil of evening primrose	3 capsules daily
Copper	5 mg daily
Magnesium orotate	300 mg daily
Manganese	5 to 10 mg a day
Niacinamide	Up to 1,000 mg daily
Lecithin	one tablespoon daily
EPA	6 to 10 grams of fish oil daily

If there are elevated triglyceride levels the requirements change a bit to include:

Chromium	2 to 300 micrograms daily
Carnitine	Anywhere from 100 to 600 mg daily
Magnesium orotate	300 mg once or twice daily
Vitamin B6	50 mg daily

Your doctor may not recommend all of these supplements or the quantities suggested. Some of the nutrients can be obtained from the diet, while others must be obtained in the form of supplements.

Healthful foods and supplements can act to shield you against the effects of the aging process. And it is men and not women who are the weaker sex. Women in the sixty-five-and-older age group constitute the fastest growing age segment of the U. S. population. It was not so in the beginning. Statistics show about 106 males are born to every one hundred females. After the first thirty or forty years the sexes are about equal but by age ninety-five a man is outnumbered four to one.

Although we are emphasizing the nutrients necessary for sexual health, such as the essential fatty acids, vitamin E, and the B complex (for sex-hormone synthesis), evening primrose oil (gamma-linolenic acid), glycine, alanine, and glutamic acid (for a healthy prostate), zinc and so on, all of the vitamins and minerals play their parts and must be a part of daily intake.

Vitamin E

We have touched on some of the attributes of vitamin A at the beginning of this chapter, and now it's time to examine the second of the oil-soluble vitamins, vitamin E.

Nutrition is a very young science. We have learned more about it in the last twenty years than in all of the time till then. For example, here are some recent findings about vitamin E: Jeffy Bland, Ph.D., University of Puget Sound, showed that vitamin E could dramatically increase the life of red blood cells. Robert S. London, M.D., of Baltimore's Sinai Hospital, found that 600 IU of vitamin E will reduce fibrocystic breast disease. Also, Doctor London has corroborated the ability of vitamin E to promote high-density lipoprotein levels. This is the type of cholesterol that is considered to be protective against heart disease.

Robert Bruce., M.D., and Elizabeth Bright-See, M.D., conducted a study with the Ontario Cancer Institute in Toronto,

Canada that confirmed earlier work showing that vitamin E protects against *the formation of nitrosamines* in the body. Nitrosamines are a powerful class of carcinogens that are formed after eating nitrate and nitrite-containing foods.

J.D. Kanofsky, M.D., of Columbia University and P. B. Kanofsky, Ph.D., of Temple University in Pennsylvania, reported evidence that vitamin E can dissolve blood clots in heart and lung tissue.

In a similar study to Dr. London's, William Hermann, Jr., M.D., of Houston's Memorial City General Hospital, has found that vitamin E supplementation will increase high-density lipids, which researchers believe will reduce heart disease risk.

From the National Cancer Institute in Bethesda, H.N. Londer, M.D., and C.E. Meyers, M.D., examined the role of vitamin E as a free radical scavenger to prevent tissue damage from lethal effects of whole-body exposure to radiation. They found that vitamin E improved overall survival and that the vitamin improved statistical survival of tissues.

The Canandian National Research Council found that vitamin E protects hormone balance and is suggested in the medical treatment of asthma, heart disease, stroke, and aging.

The essential action of vitamin E in the human body is well understood, but extremely complicated. One of its greatest feats seems to be to protect essential, unsaturated oils from premature destruction in the body. Without vitamin E, oils (also known as fats) would turn rancid—on the inside! You know what rancidity does to foods outside of the body. Consider the damaging effects when it happens inside. So, a good supply of vitamin E is essential for that reason and for many others.

Vitamin E is not one vitamin, but is a family of compounds known as tocopherols. Alpha-tocopherol is the form most widely distributed in nature and the most active of the compounds. Others are named beta, gamma, and delta.

Its antioxidant action is enhanced by other nutrients, such as vitamin C and selenium. Along with the enzymes glutathione peroxidase, catalase, and superoxide dismutaste, it protects body cells and tissues from oxidative destruction.

Tissues, such as the testes, accumulate polyunsaturated fats and are the first to deteriorate when vitamin E is deficient.

Ceroid pigmentation (a yellow-brown discoloration of tissue) accumulates over time when there is an excess of fat and a decrease in the amount of vitamin E.

As an antioxidant, vitamin E functions:

- to stabilize membranes and protect them against free radical damage
- to help protect the lungs from air pollutants
- to help prevent the growth of tumors
- to help protect the skin, eye, liver, breast, and calf muscle to prevent growing-older cramps in the legs
- to increase the body's stores of vitamin A.

If there is a deficiency, the major influence is on the reproductive organs, the nervous system, muscle tissue, and blood.

The *role of vitamin E in the prevention of premature aging* is a topic of current interest. *The theory is that aging is due to a progressive accumulation of cellular deterioration caused by free radical damage and that vitamin E retards this process.*

Brain damage in deficiency states result from the antioxidant effect of the vitamin. The peroxides, if unchecked, can alter the membrane structure of nerve cells and perhaps interfere with normal function.

Vitamin E also conserves iron by protecting erythrocytes (red blood cells) from breakdown, thus reducing the turnover rate of iron.

Tocopherols are found in plant and animal food, with vegetable seed oils being the largest contributors. Not all plant oils have the same amount of vitamin E.

Safflower oil contains ninety percent vitamin E, while corn oil has only ten percent. Vitamin E content is related to linoleic acid content. Thus, safflower oil, with a high linoleic acid content, is one of the best sources of natural vitamin E.

When white flour is milled to make white bread, most of the vitamin E is lost, and if chloride dioxide is used during the bleaching process, all of the vitamin E is lost. When vegetable oils are refined and purified, vitamin E is lost.

To get vitamin E from your diet, you have to eat whole grains, green leafy vegetables, vegetable oil that is not processed, wheat germ oil, egg yolk, butter, liver, and nuts.

As mentioned, vitamin E is useful in the treatment of intermittent claudication. This is a condition in which the blood supply to the leg muscles is reduced by arteriosclerosis or thickening of the walls of the arteries that supply these muscles with blood. The result of this inadequate supply of blood is pain, usually associated with walking.

According to Doctor Leo Gitman, senior research associate at Bethel Hospital, vitamin E has rejuvenation powers. It is capable of reducing fat in the blood. This makes it a major preventive of heart attacks and hardening of the arteries, which are regarded as "aging" problems.

Vitamin E has youth-giving power to help promote a smooth blood stream. In the *American Journal of Physiology*, Doctors Zierler, Grob, and Lilienthal tell of experiments in which they discovered that vitamin E helps reduce clots in the veins and arteries.

A smooth and free-flowing blood stream contributes to a more youthful system. Vitamin E helps to clear obstructions and promote this smooth flow. Since the blood carries nutrients to every cell and tissue, the better the flow the healthier the entire body.

According to Doctor Michael Weiner, writing with Jonathon Rothschild in "The Vitamin That Likes Oxygen," *Runner's World*, February 1980, when long-distance runners had trouble in the rarified atmosphere of Mexico City during the 1968 Olympic games (especially trouble with the nerves and long muscles of the legs), sports medicine experts found that vitamin E, by facilitating oxygen transport, was particularly beneficial.

Not only physical stress, but also nutritional stress, can be stemmed by the complex relationship between vitamin E and lipoproteins.

Also, according to the *American Journal of Clinical Nutrition*, February 1982, megadoses of vitamin E created promising effects in increasing immune responses to antigens, and improved the host resistance to microoganisms.

The combination of vitamin E, C, and selenium has an important role, demonstrated by the Linus Pauling Institute of Science and Medicine, in preventing proliferation of certain cancer cells. Cancer-causing effects of mercury, lead, and cadmium have also been mitigated by vitamin E therapy.

For the health-conscious individual, vitamin E should be an integral part of the supplementation program, but each of us has a different need, depending on our environment (smog versus clean air), our diet, and our physical makeup. Many experts recommend different amounts, because it is inappropriate to specify an exact amount for everyone's need. Given normal health, however, it is comforting to know that the vitamin is not toxic in almost any amount.

Robert Atkins, M.D., in *Nutrition Breakthrough*, tells of the basic vitamin-mineral formula he usually prescribes for most of his office patients. You will notice that the dose of vitamin E initially is given as 200 IU.

Dr. Atkins' Basic Vitamin-Mineral Prescription

Nutrient	Recommended daily allowance
Vitamin A	10,000 IU
Vitamin D	400 IU
Vitamin B1	100 mg
Vitamin B2	75 mg
Vitamin C	1,500 mg
Niacin	50 mg
Niacinamide	100 mg
Vitamin B6	200 mg
Choline	750 mg
Inositol	450 mg

Biotin	300 mcg
PABA	1,200 mg
Calcium pantothenate	150 mg
Folic acid	3.6 mg
Vitamin B12	750 mcg
Vitamin E	200 IU
Calcium	600 mg
Magnesium	300 mg
Manganese	6 mg
Zinc	45 mg
Rutin	45 mg
Bioflavonoids	300 mg
Iron (ferrous fumarate)	18 mg
Iodine (kelp)	225 mcg

Vitamin D

There's a new theory of evolution that states that all of mankind evolved from one female. That one female was a mutant whose body did things in ways that were different from all other females. Previous to her arrival on earth, we made all of our vitamins within our bodies. Even though there was loads of vitamin C available from plants, the body wasted space by manufacturing it anyway. This new female did not manufacture vitamin C, or any of the other vitamins for that matter, except vitamin D. She used the mechanism for other purposes, maybe to get smarter, think faster than the other females, mate with better males. Anyway, she survived to pass on this "new" way of living, and to this day, the only vitamin we can manufacture in quantity in our body is vitamin D. The rest must be obtained from food or supplements.

The body manufactures all of its steroid hormones from cholesterol. I hope that doesn't surprise you. After all the bad publicity about cholesterol, you find it's necessary to life.

The dermis, the skin just beneath our skin, and the sweat glands both contain quantities of a material called dehydrocholesterol. If light with just the right amount of energy strikes the dehydrocholesterol, it is changed to a substance called cholecalciferol (vitamin D3). This D3 travels to the liver to be finally turned into the vitamin D the body uses.

The vitamin D3 form is found in fish oil and in eggs. If you buy a vitamin supplement, try to find one that uses vitamin D3. It will state that on the label.

Vitamin D is both a vitamin and a hormone. Its formation in the skin is restricted by a number of qualities, such as skin pigment, keratin (which screens ultraviolet light), smog, fog, smoke, clothing, screens, and most glass. This means that most people don't get an adequate amount of sunlight because they spend most of the day indoors away from sunlight and under artificial light. Artificial light will not stimulate the production of vitamin D. In fact, owing to the amount of pollution, dust, and smog in the air, it's a wonder why we all don't have a vitamin D deficiency.

Most of us avoid the sun because we've been told that the sun's rays can cause skin cancer. However, it's the overexposure to the sun that can be a problem; but a certain amount of sunlight falling on exposed skin is necessary to life!

If you sit inside behind a glass window and let the sun play on your body you'll get warm, but you won't manufacture any vitamin D because the light coming through the window does not have the right amount of energy to change the cholesterol into the vitamin.

Vitamin D promotes calcium absorption from the intestines. That's the reason that milk with vitamin E added is such a good source of calcium. Supplements of calcium should also have some vitamin D to help the calcium into the blood stream. Vitamin D also regulates the coming and going of calcium from bones into the blood stream and from the blood stream into bones.

Vitamin D regulates calcium and phosphorus. If there is a deficiency of the vitamin, normal calcification will not occur. This is bad news for bones and teeth. A vitamin D deficiency is responsible for rickets in children and osteomalacia in adults. Celiac disease (gluten enteropathy) is indirectly related to a vitamin D deficiency.

Vitamin D is found in cod liver oil, other fish oils, the edible portions of oily fish such as salmon, herring and sardines, egg yolk, butter, and liver.

Benefits of vitamin D, once thought to be restricted to building strong bones and teeth, are now seen to be more extensive. Even mental retardation may be helped by vitamin D. The concern over calcium has furthered study into the use of this vitamin and there may be an incredible future for this oil-soluble vitamin.

Vitamin K

The last of the oil-soluble vitamins is vitamin K. Vitamin K is found naturally as vitamin D1 (found in alfalfa leaf), and vitamin K2 (produced by microorganisms in the intestinal tract of many animals). It is important to blood clotting and may also play a part in bone mineralization.

A deficiency is rare, because vitamin K is found in so many plants and animals and is synthesized in the lumen. Mineral oil, commonly used as a laxative, reduces body amounts of vitamin K by binding with the vitamin and carrying it out of the body. The use of salicylates over a long period of time can increase the need for vitamin K. Although it is usually not found in most vitamin formulas, it is easily obtained by eating dark green leafy vegetables.

The water-soluble vitamins differ from the oil-soluble vitamins in that they cannot be stored in the body. Every time you lose water you lose vitamins. They are needed on a daily basis either from food or from supplements or both.

Vitamin B1

When you take vitamin B1 (thiamin) into your body, it has to combine with phosphoric acid to make its coenzyme form called thiamin pyrophosphate (TPP). This is implicated in the synthesis of acetylcholine, the brain neurotransmitter which exerts so much control over memory, sex, and other activities.

Therefore, any program to increase your control over your own body and mind must include this important vitamin.

Vitamin B1 plays a key role in carbohydrate metabolism. If you eat more carbohydrates, you need more B1. Although we can get B1 from many foods, few of them have it in any great concentration. Lean pork, dry beans and peas, some organ meats, and some nuts have reasonable amounts; however, supplements are indicated for most diets.

Another problem in obtaining a sufficient supply of vitamin B1 from food is that it is destroyed easily by heat, water, baking soda, and other cooking ingredients and techniques.

Even a mild deficiency can lead to poor memory, instability, depression, insomnia, lack of initiative, and inability to concentrate.

Our modern, stressed society needs the nerve-calming effects of B1. It is important to the proper functioning of the peripheral nerves and can contribute to a healthy mental attitude.

Energy is the capacity of the body for doing work or its equivalent in the strict physical sense. Your energy or capacity for doing work depends on the food you eat, how you combine the foods, the type of exercise you do, how you relax, the efficiency of your digestive system and assimilative system. The nutritional calories in your food cannot be turned into energy until they reach the cells in an absorbable condition. Energy cannot be released from what you eat until the food is completely broken down in the digestive tract, absorbed through the lining of the alimentary tract, and distributed to the individual cells via the blood vessels.

Enzymes must be present in the digestion of your food, and enzymes must be present in each cell to convert food energy into cellular energy. Cellular enzymes depend on the presence of vitamins and minerals to create energy from food. If there are not enough of the needed vitamins and minerals present when food is delivered, the cells will not be able to be energized and the body will become fatigued.

The B-complex vitamins help to metabolize carbohydrates. B1 is essential as a coenzyme in liver metabolism. The mineral zinc is essential to protein digestion, while calcium is vital to the lipase enzyme in fat digestion. This illustrates the complexity of maintaining health and the need for all of the vitamins and minerals at the same time.

Vitamin B2 (riboflavin) serves as an essential respiratory enzyme in all cells and plays a vital role in the conversion of dietary protein to usable energy.

One of its other functions is the maintenance of the epithelial tissue (along with vitamin A). The skin and upper respiratory tract appear to be especially vulnerable to a deficiency. Since milk is the major provider of riboflavin, if you're not a milk drinker because you don't like it or can't digest it, chances are you are low in this nutrient.

B2 is necessary, for amino acid synthesis and cellular growth cannot take place in the absence of riboflavin. Several symptoms have been noted with an inadequate intake. These include:

- Cracks at the corner of the mouth and inflammation of the mucous membranes in the mouth
- Smooth purple-tinged tongue
- Reddening of the eyes, and eyes that tire easily, burn, itch, and are sensitive to light.

Although milk is the best source of riboflavin, other dairy products, such as cheese and yogurt, will provide substantial amounts. Oysters, meat, green vegetables, eggs, mushrooms, asparagus, broccoli, avocado, tuna, and salmon are fair sources. If you take a riboflavin supplement and it tints the urine a yellow-orange color, don't worry about it. It is a water-soluble vitamin and that's the reason we need it every day.

Vitamin B3

Without vitamin B3 (niacin), we'd all be raving lunatics! Pellagra is a disease caused by poor diet. The insanity that accompanies the condition often includes insomnia, loss of memory, depression, confusion, nervousness, anxiety and hallucinations. The cure is simple—it is the vitamin niacin.

Of course, a point to remember is that good physical and mental health demands a solid nutritional base and this requires a diet of unrefined foods rich in vitamins and minerals or supplements for insurance. Niacin is just one of the B-complex vitamins.

In *Body, Mind, and the B-Vitamins* by Ruth Adams and Frank Murray, the authors quote Doctor Abram Hoffer on the work of Doctor William Kaufman in using three to four grams of B3 a day with six hundred people suffering from arthritis. The results were fantastic. *He was able to reverse the arthritic changes which are so often associated with senility.*

CAUTION: This dose is so much higher than the RDA that it cannot be used without the constant supervision of a doctor. The use of niacin causes a "niacin flush," which is frightening but harmless. It causes the face, head, neck, upper torso, and arms to turn a bright red color and is accompanied by a sensation of warmth and tingling. This author tried only two hundred milligrams and went through one hour of the feeling with no ill effects, but, even though aware of what would happen, I was a little frightened until it wore off.

For many years Doctor Hoffer has said that much of what is believed to be senility in the elderly is simply malnutrition. Memory loss, confusion, depression in older men and women can be reversed by using adequate supplementation along with a good diet. Doctor Hoffer feels that niacin is one of the key substances in keeping the elderly mentally alert.

Niacin has other good features. Doctor Grace A. Goldsmith of Tulane University noted in the *Journal of the American Medical*

Association that niacin seems to reduce cholesterol levels and also protects against hardening of the arteries.

Poor eyesight, bad hearing, senility, loss of memory, dullness of mind, depression, arthritis, and heart disease are related to the state of blood circulation. Indeed, most human ailments are related to inadequate circulation. The river of blood that circulates through the body is the river of life.

Edwin Boyle, M.D., research director of the Miami Heart Institute, is one of the major pioneers in determining the circulatory benefits of niacin.

Ingestion of niacin causes the small blood vessels to dilate (enlarge), which promotes the flow of blood and improves the circulation. It also causes histamine to be released from the cells into the tissues of the skin. At the same time, a powerful agent is released by the mast cells that are around the blood vessels. This agent is a substance called heparin, and is produced by the body. Heparin is also present in liver, and is extracted from pig's liver in commercial quantities to be used by doctors as an anticoagulant in the prevention and treatment of thrombosis and bacterial endocarditis, postoperative pulmonary embolisms (lung clots), and in repairs of vascular injury—and you can get it free from your own body!

Both niacin and vitamin C are especially effective in strengthening all circulatory channels. It is difficult to get niacin from the diet. The body does convert some of the amino acid L-tryptophan to niacin but it is a small amount. The niacin we get from meat is in the form of niacinamide. It is useful for almost all of the jobs that niacin accomplishes, except for niacin's effect on circulation. The answer appears to be supplemental niacin. You can try taking twenty-five milligrams after a meal. Then try fifty milligrams or seventy-five to one hundred milligrams. At some time and dose-level you will experience the flush. Don't be startled, it will soon pass and give you a feeling of well-being. If you take the niacin intermittently, there will be a release of stored histamine and heparin, which the body will then build up once more. There are some indications that vitamin B2 should be taken along with large doses of niacin, plus vitamin B6 and vitamin C.

Natural sources of niacin would include sunflower seeds, rice bran syrup, whole grain products, green peas, and brewer's yeast. All of them are from the vegetable family because, as said before, meat, fish, and fowl contain the niacinamide form of vitamin B3.

Vitamin B6

Without vitamin B6 (pyridoxine), the neurotransmitters norepinephrine and acetylcholine could not be manufactured. Therefore, without this vitamin there are no sexual inclinations!

The coenzyme of pyridoxine works with phosphorylase in the conversion of glycogen to glucose. Without this enzyme, the body could not use glucose for energy.

Some drugs impair vitamin B6 absorption or utilization. These include amphetamine, chlorpromazine, reserpine, and oral contraceptive pills.

There are many causes of heart disease, but here is one you haven't heard of. It's called homocysteine and it's manufactured in your body! Homocysteine is produced in the body when protein consumption is relatively high and vitamin B6 intake is low. When protein is broken down under normal circumstance and there is an ample supply of B6, it is broken down as follows: protein—methionine—homocysteine—B6—cystathione. The cystathione is a harmless substance. However, if B6 is not present, the homocysteine is not broken down and remains in the body.

It can attack and strip away surface cells on blood vessel walls. Cholesterol is attracted to the bare sites and clumps develop. This theory is being promoted by Doctor Kilmer McCully, a professor of pathology at Harvard Medical School.

Although the RDA of vitamin B6 is two milligrams, many people do not even obtain this small amount in their diets unless they are vegetarians. Researchers, such as Doctor Richard Passwater, recommend twenty-five to fifty milligrams as a dietary safeguard.

The protective effects of vitamin B6 extend beyond the vitamin's role in blocking homocysteine formation in the body. It is a precursor to adrenaline and cortisone, two hormones that help defend the body against a variety of stresses. It is necessary for the synthesis of DNA and RNA, the nucleoproteins, and for the metabolism of fat, protein, and carboyhdrate.

B6 is found naturally in cantaloupe, tuna, lentils, whole grains, rice, bananas, spinach, potatoes, and other fruits and vegetables.

B6 and B12 can help prevent anemia, and in the Netherlands doctors say that B6 can relieve diabetic symptoms and that calcium oxalate kidney stone formation can be lowered by the use of B6 supplements. The ability of B6 to help nervous conditions was demonstrated by Doctor John M. Ellis: "In hospitals and clinics, B6 relieves certain forms of neuritis in the feet, arms, legs, and hands...edema (an excess accumulation of fluid in the tissues) can be drastically reduced by vitamin B6." Recent reports cite the ability of vitamin B6 to clear up some cases of carpel tunnel syndrome without resorting to surgery. The suggested dose was two hundred milligrams three times a day, under the care of a physician.

The B-complex vitamins are more easily destroyed by storage and processing than the fat-soluble vitamins like vitamin A. Heat, light, and drugs such as aspirin diminish the potency of B vitamins in the food you eat. Hence, you don't always get all the B vitamins that are naturally found in whole grains, vegetables, dairy products, or fruits due to losses brought about by storage, transportation, exposure to heat and also by deficiencies in your own digestive system. Alcohol and canning, roasting, or stewing meat is damaging to the B6 content. A good B-complex vitamin containing fifty milligrams of each of the B vitamins (B12, folic acid, and biotin are expressed in micrograms usually; B12, one hundred micrograms; folic acid, four hundred micrograms; biotin, ten micrograms) can be taken once or twice a day. If you intend to use higher doses therapeutically to halt or reverse an existing condition, it would be wise to contact a nutrition-oriented physician with experience in using orthomolecular doses.

Vitamin B12

Vitamin B12 is unique among all of the other vitamins. It is the only vitamin that combines a mineral in its molecule. Usually we speak of minerals as being separate, but equal in value to vitamins. Zinc, selenium, calcium, and so on, stand alone in importance and in use, but here is a vitamin that actually incorporates a mineral into its structure. That mineral is cobalt.

When B12 is manufactured in the laboratory, it is called cyanocobalamin. That's because a cyanide radical attaches to the B12 during manufacture. It is not found that way in nature, but is due to contamination.

However, that's the way almost all of the B12 is found in the vitamin formulas.

Some companies manufacture a B12 called hydroxycobalamin. It is free from the contamination of cyanide, and may be better for you.

B12 helps in the manufacture of one of the body's protective amino acids called L-methionine, which is needed in the choline system. That's the system involved in memory and nerve transmission.

It is also involved in many critical body functions, including the protection of the insulation around nerves, called the myelin sheath, and the prevention of anemia.

A deficiency is common in later life, and can be corrected by adequate supplementation.

Good food sources of B12 are organ meats (liver, heart, kidney), clams, oysters, crab, salmon, sardines, and egg yolk.

Pantothenic acid or calcium pantothenate is involved in the adrenal gland production of stimulating hormones, along with vitamin C. It also functions in the production of the neurotransmitter acetylcholine.

It is converted to coenzyme A in the body. Without it the steroid hormones could not be manufactured and sex would be nonexistent.

Good food sources include liver and organ meats, fish, chicken, eggs, cheese, sweet potatoes, green peas, and dried beans.

Folic Acid

A deficiency of this vitamin is most common in the United States. The symptoms resemble that of a B12 deficiency, except that lack of folic acid doesn't have the terrible effects on nerves that the B12 lack will have. It's easy to be in need of folic acid, because the vitamin can be destroyed by improper storage of foods. It can also disappear when cooking water is discarded, or if foods are overcooked or reheated.

B12 and folic acid are usually found together in vitamin supplement formulas. If your formula does not contain them, get another brand.

Vitamin C

This vitamin helps keep your skin looking younger because it is deeply involved in forming collagen, the cementing tissue that holds you together. It helps prevent bruising, builds amino acids and hormones. It contributes to the formation of tyrosine in the body, which forms the neurotransmitters noradrenaline and norepinephrine. It helps the adrenal glands combat stress and provide the energy for lovemaking.

Vitamin C is one of the principal elements in helping to rid the body of excess cholesterol.

This is not a book solely about vitamins and minerals, but a little background about some of them is helpful. There are many books that go into the part vitamins and minerals play in good health and good sex, and you should read them.

One book is *Vitamins and You*, by Robert J. Benowicz. It's written in plain language and overs all of the vitamins, minerals, and other nutrients. Nutrition and the intake of vitamins and minerals affect the endocrine glands and, in turn, these glands affect the strength of the sex drive.

Before leaving the story of vitamins and minerals, we have to mention the mineral phosphorus.

It is the first mineral that was discovered to be linked to sexual arousal.

The workers who refined phosphorus were in a constant state of erection, but, don't think you can take raw phosphorus and solve all of your problems. It's too easy to get a toxic dose and then that erection will be your last one!

Take it in supplement form, as found in your vitamin formula, or eat fish, eggs, milk, nuts, seeds, and beans.

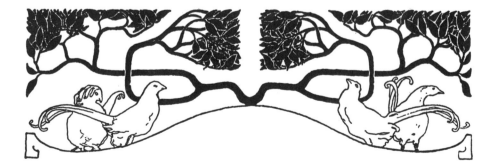

Erotic Cookery

There are many valuable dishes that provide considerable energy and act as nutritional stimulants. Some of these will be described here, along with a one-week erotic menu designed to begin your food foray into an improved sexual jungle.

When oil is called for, use sunflower, safflower, or corn oil. Limit your intake of caffeine, salt, refined sugar (you can substitute fructose), and refined flour.

This recipe combines the *concentrated virility foods* eggs, honey, and milk in a delightful drink.

Right Into Bed Egg Flip

1 egg yolk
½ pint milk
pinch of salt
1 small glass brandy or sherry
1 teaspoon honey

Beat the egg in the milk until frothy. Allow the foam to settle. Add salt, brandy, and honey. Whip again and serve. Sip slowly. For a stronger result you can use two egg yolks.

Notice how well you can combine erotic foods to make a complete meal. In this recipe you combine eggs, paprika, and fresh mushrooms, all designed by nature to influence sexuality.

Mushroom Savoury

½ pound fresh mushrooms
Paprika
Rye toast
1 egg
Salt
Boiled peas
Breadcrumbs

Beat the egg with 1 level teaspoon of breadcrumbs. Dice the mushrooms. Add pinch of salt and two pinches of paprika to mushrooms. Mix the mushrooms with the eggs and breadcrumbs. Then put the mixture into a greased pan and sautee. Serve with hot, boiled peas on rye toast. Grilled kidneys can be added, or sausage or bacon.

You can utilize the power of organ meats with this very enjoyable mixture. Even people who would never sit down to a meal of organ meat will eat this combination with delight.

Mixed Grill

Kidneys
Sweetbreads
Liver
Mushrooms
Small boiled new potatoes
Hardboiled eggs, sliced
Grilled tomatoes
Peas tossed in fresh creamery butter
Salt and pepper to taste

Lightly saute kidneys, sweetbreads, and liver with salt and pepper to taste. Serve on a warm platter, garnished with mushrooms, potatoes, sliced hardboiled eggs, grilled tomatoes, and peas.

Not all erotic combinations appear to be familiar. For example:

Heart's Tart

Chop up a large onion.
Mince a clove or two of garlic.
Line a small pie tin with pastry.

Lay in the onion and the garlic and add a little paprika. Follow with a layer of cooked bacon and cover with a pastry crust. Bake in a hot oven until pastry is brown. Serve with spears of asparagus and cauliflower.

This is an unusual fish dish which combines fish, milk, and eggs to add up to another stimulating meal.

Tempting Timbales

Butter, softened
2 additional tablespoons butter
¼ cup bread crumbs
¾ cup milk
1 cup minced cooked fish or shellfish (any white fish, or shrimp or crab)
1 tablespoon minced parsley
1/8 teaspoon dried dill
2 eggs, slightly beaten
Salt to taste
Freshly ground pepper
¼ teaspoon lemon juice

Generously butter 4 custard cups. Melt the 2 tablespoons butter, add bread crumbs and milk. Cook over medium heat for 5 minutes, stirring constantly. Add the fish, parsley, dill, and eggs. Season with salt, pepper, and lemon juice. Fill each custard cup about two-thirds full. Place them in a pan of hot water that comes about two-thirds of the way up the sides of the cups. Bake at 350 degrees for about 20 minutes. Remove, and let stand for 5 minutes. Run a knife around the inside of each cup and unmold onto a warm platter. Surround with a white sauce or other favorite sauce. Serve with green beans.

Unusual combinations can offer the best in love-cookery. This one sounds strange but is very tasty.

Banana Beefsteak

¾ pound beefsteak
3 bananas
Flour
1 ounce butter
1 teaspoon olive oil
Salt and pepper to taste

Remove excess fat from the meat and brush it with melted butter or olive oil. Saute beef until cooked in the usual manner. Slice the bananas thickly and dip them in flour. They may also be sprinkled lightly with cinnamon. Fry bananas in the butter until golden brown. Serve beef surrounded by bananas and raw sliced tomatoes.

Here is a recipe for liver that will tempt most people and will add organ meat to the menu. This dish combines liver with eggs, and adds milk for good measure.

Liver Florentine

1 large slice of liver
1 medium onion
1 tablespoon oil
2 eggs
Milk, butter, salt, pepper, and cinnamon
Fingers of crisp toast

Put the oil in a frying pan and slightly fry the chopped onion. Add liver in thin slices and fry. Scramble the eggs (with a little milk) in butter. Add salt, pepper, and cinnamon to taste immediately before cooking. Serve the fried liver and onion on a base of scrambled egg and crisp toast.

This is from *Venus in the Kitchen*, edited by Norman Douglas. What more could any man ask for as a strengthening agent?

Love Potion

    6 large egg yolks
    1 glass Madeira
    1 cup cold chicken broth
    1 teaspoon cinnamon

Beat the six egg yolks, slowly adding the Madeira. Beat in the chicken broth and the cinnamon. Strain into an earthenware pot and cook gently, stirring constantly. Add a pat of butter. As it thickens, pour into cups. Serve hot with a sprinkling of nutmeg and sugar.

If an opportunity presents itself and you'd like to have a roll in the hay, but have a limited time for fortification, try the following:

Bottoms Up!

    Into a small glass pour ¼ glass maraschino liqueur
    Add 1 egg yolk (do not break)
    Add:
    ¼ glass Madeira
    ¼ glass creme de cacao
    ¼ glass good brandy

Do not stir. Drink at one gulp. If it doesn't work out, have another and you won't care!

End a meal with Eve's Apples and begin a sexual encounter.

Take two large apples, core them and slice thinly. Juice an orange and blend with 4 teaspoons honey and a dash of brandy.

Pour the dressing over the apple slices and garnish with raisins, walnuts, and fresh cherries.

Frog legs have earned a reputation as aphrodisiacs. This recipe will earn you a reputation as a gourmet cook. Eat this and get ready to "spring" into bed. You'll know why frog legs are such a hot item on the French menu.

Frogs Do It!

    36 frog legs
    12 mushrooms, chopped
    4 shallots, minced
    2 ounces butter
    1 tablespoon flour
    Salt, pepper, and nutmeg to taste
    1 glass white wine
    1 cup consomme
    4 egg yolks
    2 tablspoons heavy cream

Toss frog legs for six minutes in a saucepan with mushrooms, shallots, and butter. Add flour. Season with salt, pepper, and nutmeg. Stir in white wine and consomme. Simmer for ten minutes, or until done. Remove the legs and set aside. Thicken sauce with the egg yolks mixed with cream. Return legs to sauce. Serve hot.

All products from the sea are stimulants. This scallop dish adds egg yolks and spices to improve the impetus, and it tastes good, too!

Saucy Scallops

¾ pound scallops
2 slices crustless bread
1-1 ½ tablespoons milk
½ small onion
Salt to taste

Pepper
2 eggs, lightly beaten
1 to 2 tablespoons flour
Fine, dry bread crumbs
Butter and olive oil

Soak bread in the milk. Put scallops, onion, and milk-soaked bread through a mincer. Season to taste. Add enough egg to make mixture easy to shape into patties. Dip in flour, then in remaining egg. Dip into bread crumbs to coat. Saute in butter and olive oil until golden and cooked through. Keep warm.
Create your own special sauce! Mash 4 hard-boiled eggs with the following, in amounts to suit your taste: minced dates, minced onion, honey, cumin, marjoram, mustard, vinegar, sesame oil, Worchestershire sauce, and anchovy paste. The sauce should resemble mayonnaise in consistency. Serve on top of patties.

Both participants should partake of this dish if they intend to partake of other delights later!

Roasted Garlic

20 large cloves garlic, peeled
3 tablespoons butter
1-½ tablespoon peanut oil
1-½ tablespoon olive oil
Salt and pepper to taste

Mix all ingredients in a small casserole. Bake at 350 degrees for 20 minutes. Stir and baste often. The result is a sweet, soft vegetable that will surprise the taste buds.

You will be surprised at the large amount of energy this next simple dish will engender. The protein from the eggs and the carbohydrate from the noodles combine to wake you up and pick you up at the same time.

Chinese Egg Drop Soup

    1 pint of stock
    Salt and pepper to taste
    2 eggs
    ½ teaspoon butter
    2 tablespoons previously cooked noodles

Heat the stock to boiling. Beat eggs well with a whisk and slowly add to stock, being sure to stir constantly. Add the butter and noodles while keeping the mixture at a simmer. Simmer to develop flavor and serve piping hot.

One Week Erotic Menu Plan

Monday

Breakfast:
    Oatmeal with milk and a sliced banana
    Bran muffin lightly buttered
    Herb tea

Lunch:
    Lettuce, tomato, cucumber, parsley, and green pepper salad
    3 ounces sliced turkey breast
    Carrots and brussels sprouts
    Baked potato with yogurt dressing
    Fresh pineapple
    Herb tea

Dinner:
    Vegetable-lentil soup
    Individual can of salmon (eat the bones)
    Fresh rolls
    ½ cantaloupe
    Handful of grapes

Herb tea

Snack before bedtime:
   Apple slices dipped in honey

Tuesday

Breakfast:
   Poached egg
   Whole wheat toast
   Fresh orange
   Yogurt with some fresh nuts
   Herb tea

Lunch:
   Broiled fish
   Broccoli and carrots
   ½ grapefruit
   Fresh rolls
   Herb tea

Dinner:
   Split pea soup
   London broil
   Cauliflower and beets
   Fresh green salad
   Herb tea

Snack:
   Celery sticks filled with peanut butter

Wednesday

Breakfast:
   Orange juice
   Yogurt over mango slices sprinkled with nuts
   Toast and herb tea

Lunch:
    Grilled Swiss cheese sandwich
    Green salad with oil and apple cider vinegar dressing
    Fresh grapes
    Herb tea

Dinner:
    Tomato juice cocktail
    Shrimp Creole over steamed brown rice
    Raw vegetable salad (fresh tomato, celery, zucchini, and carrots)
    Papaya or pineapple slices
    Herb tea

Snack:
    Crackers and cheese

Thursday

Breakfast:
    Avocado and banana mix (Take equal parts of avocado and ripe banana and blend well, sprinkle ground almonds on top.)
    Crackers and herb tea

Lunch:
    Pineapple and cottage cheese
    Crackers
    Herb tea

Dinner:
    Vegetable soup
    Broiled veal chops
    Green salad
    Fresh fruit in season

Snack:
    Crackers and peanut butter

Friday

    Breakfast:
    Fresh orange or grapefruit
    Scrambled eggs with bacon or sausage
    Herb tea

Lunch:
    Tomato juice
    Chef's salad (turkey and cheese)
    Rolls
    Yogurt and fruit
    Herb tea

Dinner:
    Barley soup
    Boiled lobster
    Sweet potato and green beans
    Herb tea

Snack:
    Fruit salad sprinkled with seeds and nuts

Saturday

Breakfast:
    Cottage cheese, sliced banana and pineapple
    Toast and herb tea

Lunch:

    Tangerine juice

    Liver and onions

    Fresh green salad

    Herb tea

Dinner:

    Tomato juice with lemon

    Broiled swordfish with peppers and onions

    Brown rice

    Fresh green salad topped with mushrooms

    Baked apple sprinkled with sunflower and sesame seeds

    Herb tea

Snack:

    Popcorn with a trace of salt and butter

Sunday

Breakfast:

    Sliced papaya and prunes with yogurt

    Cooked wheat cereal with milk

    Herb tea

Lunch:

    Yankee bean soup

    Fresh green salad with tuna or salmon

    Grapefruit sections

Herb tea

Dinner:
    Roast chicken
    Stir-fried vegetables (Chinese cabbage, pea pods, mushrooms,
    garlic, ginger, bamboo shoots, and cauliflower)
    Brown rice
    Herb tea

Snack:
    Melon in season, topped with crunchy nuts

You and Your Medication

You can't be sexually dominant unless you're in good health.

Most of the time "good health" rests on a foundation of carefully chosen food, adequate rest, exercise, lots of clear drinking water, vitamin and mineral supplementation, and the avoidance of pollutants.

Sometimes we have to take prescription drugs.

Sometimes those prescription drugs can hinder erectile capacity.

Some blood pressure drugs do more than lower pressure; they can cause impotence.

Just what you need to calm you down: The inability to get it up!

If this happens to you, don't panic and don't stop taking your medicine.

Discuss it with your doctor. He'll change the drug or change the dose.

In almost all of the cases, that's all that is needed.

We live in a youth-oriented culture where sex for the over-forty set is looked upon as unnecessary, maybe even a bit perverse, and, to some, just downright silly.

However, how does an action that is perfectly natural, healthy, and pursued with such abandon in youth and middle age suddenly change character and become something else?

That's like suddenly telling you that your favorite color no longer is blue and that from now on you have to wear only black.

Or, after all of the years that you have been voting the straight Democractic party you now have to vote Republican; that is, if they let you vote at all!

Studies show that people who have been interested in sex and have been sexually active all of their lives maintain that interest well into their most mature years.

But, while the spirit may be willing, the way the body responds to sexual stimulus can gradually slow down as aging progresses.

Concentrated virility foods can reverse that slowdown for the most part.

Fully fifty to seventy percent of seventy-year-old men have been found to maintain active sexual function.

Older men have found that erections occur more slowly, are less powerful and disappear more quickly after lovemaking. They also are less easily aroused the second time and it may take a bit longer. Ejaculation is less forceful and less plentiful in fluid content.

These are normal changes that can be altered with nutrition and supplements plus a choice of diet.

Certain illnesses, such as diabetes, depression, thyroid disorder, and atherosclerosis, can cause sexual problems.

So can tranquilizers.

So can abuse of alcohol or narcotics.

Older women who have led active sex lives continue to maintain a healthy interest in sex.

Some physical problems that do occur are the thinning of the vaginal wall and a decrease in vaginal lubrication. Lubrication can be increased as shown in this book and also with estrogen replacement therapy.

More women have given up sex because of a loss of partners rather than a loss of interest or ability!

Do not accept the idea that sexual dysfunction is a normal consequence of aging.

It isn't.

Barring organic or pharmacological problems, there is no reason for chronology to dictate changes in a life-long attitude towards sex.

Sex is a life-enriching process!

About The Author

William H. Lee, R.Ph., Ph.D., is a master herbalist, a registered pharmacist, and has his doctorate in nutrition. He has written numerous books and articles for the professional health field, as well as for the general public.

His monthly column, "On Nutrition," appears in *American Druggist Magazine.*

His writings include: *The Question and Answer Book of Vitamins, Herbs and Herbal Medicine, The Medical Benefits of Mushrooms, Pre-Menstrual Syndrome, The Vitamin Robbers,* and many more.

A FEW SHORT YEARS AGO
THIS ENCYCLOPEDIA OF
CONCENTRATED VIRILITY FOODS
COULDN'T HAVE BEEN WRITTEN.

All of us, of course, have heard of natural aphrodisiacs. We have all read newspaper accounts of members of royalty, and of fabulously rich men, who owed their recovery from impotence to such remedies. But it is only since the late 1970's that the nutritional and medical sciences have discovered the amazing new techniques of compressing and condensing the active ingredients in these natural aphrodisiacs so they would become far more powerful and predictable.

Now at last such concentrated natural aphrodisiacs are medicinally and nutritionally tested. They are waiting for you—to give you the kind of benefits that even dangerous drugs could never promise you before.

Here is just one example from a chapter in the book:

This substance has been renowned as an aphrodisiac and an effective remedy for human impotence for centuries. But all this was considered by many to be a folk tale...that is until truly scientific studies could begin...

By now, Stanford University has called it a "true aphrodisiac" and Science Digest *has heralded it as "a cure for impotence"...*

It is really a drug. It is thus able to penetrate the blood-brain barrier. When its potency is intensified the way you are shown, its effects usually come to full bloom in 45 minutes to an hour. There is not only an increase in blood flow to the sexual organs, but actual stimulation of the spinal nerve-clusters which control erectile tissue...

Bibliography

Adams, Ruth, and Frank Murray. *All You Should Know About Health Foods*. Atlanta, GA: Communication Channels, 1983.

— *Body, Mind and the B-Vitamins*. New York: Pinnacle Books, 1975.

— *The Good Seeds, the Rich Grains, the Hardy Nuts for a Healthier, Happier Life*. Atlanta, GA:Communication Channels, 1977.

Airola, Paavo. *Health Secrets from Europe*. New York: Arco Publishing Inc., 1971.

— *How to Get Well*. Scottsdale, AZ: Health Plus Publishers, 1987.

— *The Miracle of Garlic*. Scottsdale, AZ: Health Plus Publishers, 1987.

— *Worldwide Secrets for Staying Young*. Scottsdale, AZ: Health Plus Publishers, 1982.

Atkins, Robert, M.D. *Dr. Atkins' Nutrition Breakthrough: How to Treat Your Medical Condition Without Drugs*. New York: Bantam Books Inc., 1982.

A Barefoot Doctor's Manual: *The American Translation of the Official Chinese Paramedical Manual*. Philadelphia: Running Press Book Publishers, 1977.

Benowicz, Robert J. *Vitamins and You*. New York: Berkely Publishing Group, 1984.

Bey, Pilaff. *Venus in the Kitchen or Love's Cookery Book*. Edited by Norman Douglas. London: William Heinemann Ltd., 1952.

Brillat-Savarin, Anthelme. *Physiology of Taste*. Translated by M.F.K. Fishcr. San Diego, CA: Harcourt Brace Jovanovich, 1978.

Brooks, Marvin, and Sally Brooks. *Lifelong Lover*. New York: Doubleday Publishing Co., 1986.

Cheraskin, E., and W.M. Ringsdorff, Jr. *Psychodietetics*. New York: Bantam Books Inc., 1976.

Colbin, Annemarie. *Food and Healing*. New York: Ballantine/Del Rey/Fawcett Books, 1986.

Colgan, Michael. *Your Personal Vitamin Profile: A Medical Scientist Shows You How to Chart Your Individual Vitamin and Mineral Formula*. New York: William Morrow & Co., Inc., 1982.

Culpeper, Nicholas. *Complete Herbal*. Cedar Knolls, NJ: Wehman, 1970.

— *Culpeper's Color Herbal*. New York: Sterling Publishing Co., Inc., 1983.

Cureton, Thomas Kirk. *Physiological Effects of Wheat Germ Oil on Humans in Exercise: Forty-two Physical Training Programs Utilizing 894 Humans*. Springfield, IL: Charles C. Thomas, Publisher, 1972.

Dioscorides, Pedanius. *The Greek Herbal of Dioscorides*. New York: Hafner/Macmillan, 1959.

Fredericks, Carlton. *Carlton Fredericks' Program for Living Longer*. New York: Simon & Schuster Inc., 1983.

— *Food Facts and Fallacies*. New York: Arco Publishing Inc., 1968.

Gottlieb, Adam. *Sex Drugs and Aphrodisiacs*. San Francisco: 20th Century Alchemist/High Times/Level Press, 1974.

Heffern, Richard. *Complete Book of Ginseng*. Berkeley, CA: Celestial Arts/Ten Speed Press, 1976.

Kugler, Hans J. *Slowing Down the Aging Process*. New York: Pyramid Publications, 1973.

Lesser, Michael, M.D. *Nutrition and Vitamin Therapy*. New York: Bantam Books Inc., 1981.

Lust, John. *The Herb Book*. New York: Bantam Books Inc., 1974.

Mannerberg, Don, M.D., and June Roth. *Aerobic Nutrition*. New York: Berkley Publishing Group, 1983.

Mindell, Earl. *Earl Mindell's New and Revised Vitamin Bible*. New York: Warner Books Inc., 1985.

— *Shaping Up With Vitamins*. New York: Warner Books Inc., 1985.

Nittler, Alan H., M.D. *A New Breed of Doctor*. New York: Pyramid Publications, 1972.

Ovid. *The Art of Love*. Translated by Rolfe Humphries. Bloomington, IN: Indiana University Press, 1957.

Passwater, Richard A. *Supernutrition*. New York: Pocket Books, 1975.

Pearson, Durk, and Sandy Shaw. *Life Extension*. New York: Warner Books Inc., 1983.

The Perfumed Garden for the Soul's Delectation. Translated from the Arabic ofg the Shaykh al Nafzawi by Sir Richard F. Burton. London: Spearman, 1981.

Robinson, William J., M.D. *Treatment of Sexual Impotence in Men and Women.* New York: Eugenics Publishing Company, 1931.

Scala, James. *Making the Vitamin Connection.* New York: Harper & Row, Publishers, Inc., 1985.

Steiner, Claude M., Ph.D. *When a Man Loves a Woman: Sexual and Emotional Literacy for the Modern Man.* New York: Grove Press, 1986.

Stekel, Wilhelm. *Impotence in the Male.* New York: Liveright/W.W. Norton, 1971.

Tierra, Michael. *The Way of Herbs.* New York: Washington Square Press, 1980.

Van de Velde, Theodoor H. *Ideal Marriage: Its Physiology and Technique.* Second Edition. Edited by Margaret Smyth. Westport, CT: Greenwood Press, 1980.

Vatsyayana. *Kama Sutra.* Translated by Sir Richard Burton. Winchester, MA: Allen & Unwin Inc., 1981.

Vaughan, William J. *Low Salt Secrets for Your Diet.* New York: Warner Books Inc., 1984.

Venette, Nicholas. *Conjugal Love: or the Pleasures of the Marriage Bed.* New York: Garland Publishing Inc., 1984.

Wade, Carlson. *Bee Pollen and Your Health.* New Canaan, CT: Keats Publishing Inc., 1978.

— *Carlson Wade's Amino Acids Book.* New Canaan, CT: Keats Publishing Inc., 1985.

— *Health Tonics, Elixirs and Potions for the Look and Feel of Youth.* New York: Arco Publishing Inc., 1973.

— *Lecithin Book.* New Canaan, CT: Keats Publishing Inc., 1980.

— *Vitamins, Minerals and Other Supplements.* New Canaan, CT: Keats Publishing Inc., 1983.

Williams, Roger J. *Nutrition Against Disease.* White Plains, NY: Pitman/Longman Inc., 1971.

— *A Physician's Handbook on Orthomolecular Medicine.* New Canaan, CT: Keats Publishing Inc., 1979.

Index